ESSENTIAL LIFE SKILLS FOR GIRLS

Essential Life Skills for Girls

EVERYTHING YOU NEED TO KNOW TO THRIVE AT HOME, AT SCHOOL, AND OUT IN THE WORLD

LISA QUIRK WEINMAN AND
MEGAN MONAGHAN

ILLUSTRATED BY MARTHA SUE COURSEY

 ZEITGEIST · NEW YORK

To our younger selves and young women everywhere.
May you feel empowered and independent.

Published in the United States by Zeitgeist Young Adult, an imprint of Zeitgeist™, a division of Penguin Random House LLC, New York.
zeitgeistpublishing.com

Zeitgeist™ is a trademark of Penguin Random House LLC
ISBN: 9780593690420
Ebook ISBN: 9780593886519

Illustrations by Martha Sue Coursey
Book design by Emma Hall
Lisa Quirk Weinman's photograph © by Sam Weinman
Megan Monaghan's photograph © by John Willey

Printed in the United States of America
1st Printing

CONTENTS

PUT YOUR BEST FOOT FORWARD

YOU MIGHT THINK of learning as something you *have* to do. But learning new skills has endless benefits, even if it's just learning how to do things around the house. Why? Well, you get to decide how it will help you. Do you like to return to your room after school and see that you already made your bed? Do you want to be able to change the battery in the remote so you can watch Netflix? The more you know how to do, the more power you'll have over your life!

We are two middle school teachers and for almost 10 years, we worked in classrooms across the hallway from one another. We became great friends and both love working with students, helping them feel empowered, confident, and capable. We're excited to bring you this book so you can feel empowered and confident, too.

We realize that growing up can be hard. There are lots of awkward moments, questions, and things to learn. Our hope is that there will also be a lot of satisfaction and joy, especially when you master some of the skills in this book. Feeling confident in one skill helps you feel more confident to try another. Over time, as you explore new skills, take risks, and speak up, you'll see how even though something may feel hard at first, it gets easier with practice.

Imagine being able to say, "Sew a button? No problem. Change a lightbulb? I've got it." Challenge yourself to learn as many skills as possible and feel the satisfaction of checking them off as you master each one!

We hope you enjoy reading this book as much as we enjoyed writing it. Let's get learning!

LIFE SKILLS CHECKLIST

- Pack your lunch
- Make your bed
- Set the table
- Change a lightbulb
- Take care of your pet
- Sew a button
- Tighten a screw
- Change batteries
- Sort clothes
- Wash clothes
- Remove laundry stains
- Dry clothes
- Iron clothes
- Fold laundry
- Clean shoes/wash sneakers
- Wash and put away dishes
- Sweep, Swiffer, mop
- Vacuum
- Dust
- Take out the trash
- Clean the bathroom sink and mirror
- Clean the shower and tub
- Clean the toilet
- Use a plunger
- Use kitchen tools
- Use kitchen appliances
- Put out a kitchen fire

- Cut an onion
- Boil pasta
- Sleep tight
- Move your body
- Eat right
- Adopt healthy habits
- Practice first aid
- Visit the doctor
- Visit the dentist/ orthodontist
- Cope with stress
- Understand your emotions
- Think and respond
- Shower and shave
- Keep body odor away
- Care for your skin
- Care for your hair
- Care for your ears and nails
- Protect your teeth
- Keep a schedule
- Set up for school success
- Master homework
- Ask for help
- Resolve conflicts with authority figures
- Have a good conversation
- Show empathy
- Apologize
- Resolve conflicts

- Set and keep healthy boundaries
- Deal with group conflicts
- Use social media wisely
- Enjoy time alone
- Spend wisely
- Save wisely
- Budget
- Understand and manage a bank account
- Leave a tip
- Donate
- Communicate online
- Make and receive phone calls
- Text with care
- Email with care
- Write a thank-you note
- Use good manners
- Read a map
- Pack a suitcase
- Host a hangout
- Be a great guest
- Watch a younger child
- Pick and wrap a present
- Make smart decisions

PART ONE
AT HOME

This first part of the book is filled with instructions for skills that will help you to become independent. Part of being independent means taking good care of yourself and your belongings. This takes time and practice! In this chapter you'll learn everything from how to pack a delicious lunch to how to change a lightbulb. By the time you finish reading, you'll be capable of so many new skills that will hopefully inspire confidence and independence!

CHAPTER 1
AROUND THE HOUSE

- [ ] PACK YOUR LUNCH

- [ ] MAKE YOUR BED

- [ ] SET THE TABLE

- [ ] CHANGE A LIGHTBULB

- [ ] TAKE CARE OF YOUR PET

- [ ] SEW A BUTTON

- [ ] TIGHTEN A SCREW

- [ ] CHANGE BATTERIES

PACK YOUR LUNCH

Lunchtime is a chance to fuel up before tackling the afternoon ahead. But let's face it—a soggy sandwich and brown apples feel bleak. So why not pack a lunch that becomes the highlight of your day? Think about foods you like, and ask your caregivers to take you grocery shopping to stock up on favorites.

1. **Begin with proteins.** Proteins are your superpower! They provide long-lasting energy to help you conquer the day. Here are some protein-rich options:

   - Hummus and crackers
   - Cheese
   - Hard-boiled egg
   - Pizza
   - Nuts or nut butter
   - Popcorn
   - Yogurt

2. **Add color.** Color adds visual appeal and nutritional variety. Add a rainbow of fruits and veggies and bring some ranch dressing for dipping, if you like. Colorful ideas include:

   - Apples or pears
   - Carrots or celery
   - Clementines or oranges
   - Mini cucumbers
   - Bananas
   - Berries
   - Watermelon
   - Sliced peppers

3. **Treat yourself!** After working hard all morning, it feels good to reward yourself with food you love. Treats can be sweet or not! Some recipe ideas for treats include:

   - Oatmeal chocolate-chip muffins
   - Protein or fruit smoothie
   - Trail mix
   - Quesadillas
   - Fruit salad
   - Mac and cheese
   - Energy bars or balls

MAKE YOUR BED

We hear you—why make your bed? It's only going to get messed up again later, right? Well, here are a few good reasons to straighten those sheets: Research shows that people sleep better when they crawl into crisply made beds, and sleep is incredibly important to being happy and healthy. And making your bed increases your productivity throughout the day. By completing that one task, you've started the momentum to complete other small jobs. In other words, making your bed is one small step that starts a chain reaction of accomplishment!

1. **Start with a clean slate.** Begin by making sure your sheets are clean and fresh. Clear away stuffed animals, books, and crumbs.

2. **Straighten the sheets.** Tighten the bottom sheet and pull up the top flat sheet from the foot of the bed. Make sure it's smooth and straight. Pull up any blankets so they cover the sheets (or lay the blanket a little lower than the sheets).

3. **Fold and tuck.** Fold over the top of the top sheet and blankets 6 to 12 inches (or just the top sheet if the blankets lie lower than the sheet). Tuck the bottoms of the sheets and blankets under the sides of the mattress.

4. **Make smooth moves.** Lay any bedspread or comforter evenly over the bed. Make sure it reaches the top of the bed. Smooth it out and make it look as inviting as possible.

5. **Pop on the pillows.** Grab your pillows and give them a good fluff, making them as plump and comfy as a marshmallow cloud. Arrange the pillows at the top of the bed.

There you have it: a well-made and welcoming bed! You've set the stage for a great day ahead. Plus, you now have a cozy space to snuggle into at the end of the day. Sleep tight!

SET THE TABLE

Setting the table is a thoughtful way to help the person cooking dinner. If you're in the mood, you can really dish out some style by using colorful placemats, folding napkins in creative ways, or finding pretty flowers or a quirky centerpiece as a conversation starter.

SUPPLIES:

- Placemats or tablecloth
- Plates
- Napkins
- Forks, knives, spoons
- Glasses

1. **Lay the foundation.**
   Clear and wipe down the table. Drape the tablecloth evenly over the table, or if using placemats, set one down in front of each chair.

2. **Plate it up.** Set a plate in the center of each placemat. Fold a napkin and tuck it next to the plate on the left side.

3. **Get fancy with flatware.** Place the fork over the napkin on the left side. Set the knife (blade facing inward) on the right, and set the spoon to the right of the knife.

4. **Sparkle and shine.** Place a glass above the knife on the right side (unless that person is a lefty!).

To help even more, ask your caregiver what condiments are needed. For example, if they're making spaghetti, you can put grated Parmesan cheese on the table. Taco Tuesday? Put out bowls of fixings. You get the picture!

CHANGE A LIGHTBULB

Brighten up everyone's day by changing lightbulbs when they burn out. These steps will "shed some light" on how to get the job done!

1. Find a lightbulb that matches the size and shape of the one that went out.

2. Choose the best lightbulb for your space and the environment.

   - Wattage: Lightbulbs have different amounts of power, or wattage. Lightbulbs with lower wattages use less power and are more energy efficient.

   - Types of lightbulbs: In the past, incandescent lightbulbs were most common in homes, but now LED lights are recommended because they're more energy efficient.

3. Turn the power off by flicking the wall switch or lamp switch to the off position. For extra safety, unplug the entire light fixture.

4. Make sure the old lightbulb is cool to touch—sometimes it gets very hot. Once it's cool, unscrew the old bulb.

5. Safely dispose of the old bulb by wrapping it in the new bulb's packaging or a paper towel. Place it carefully in the garbage or give it to an adult for recycling.

6. Screw in the new lightbulb, turn on the power, flick on the light switch, and *voilà*!

TAKE CARE OF YOUR PET

Caring for a pet can feel overwhelming, but wow, it is also such a wonderful experience! We'll talk about caring for dogs and cats here—ask your veterinarian about caring for other types of pets.

WHAT DOES YOUR DOG OR CAT NEED?

- **Water.** Pets should always have access to water. Refill the water bowl daily with clean, cold water.

- **Food.** Ask your caregivers or the veterinarian what (and when) your pet should eat, and how much food is required. Make sure the food bowl is accessible to them. Avoid feeding pets from the table! And avoid toxic foods (for dogs, this includes chocolate, onions, and raisins, to name a few).

- **Safety.**

  - On warm days, make sure your pet has shade and water if they are outside. If it's cold or snowy, watch the temperature and don't leave your pet outside too long.

  - Make sure your pet is protected from cars and other animals.

  - Ask your caregiver about getting your pet an ID tag and microchip.

- **Exercise and play.** Ask how much exercise your pet needs. Exercise makes a big difference in an animal's mental and physical health. Taking your dog for a walk and playing together is good for you, too!

- **Bathroom breaks.** Cats need a litter box that is cleaned daily. Dogs need to be taken outside at least three times a day; more often for some dogs (and puppies!). Ask an adult how often to walk or take out your dog. A regular routine can help you and your pet both know what to expect.

- **Healthcare.** Pets get checkups just like people and might need an occasional shot or vitamins. Some pets also visit a groomer to have their hair or fur cared for and get their nails cut.

SEW A BUTTON

A button falling off your favorite shirt doesn't mean it's ruined. Replace or repair it so you can wear your shirt again!

1. Gather your materials: scissors, thread, a sewing needle, and a button.

2. Cut a 16-inch piece of thread. Slide the thread through the eye of the needle and pull it through so both ends are even. Tie the two ends together.

3. Pull the needle up through the back of the fabric into one of the holes of the button. Push the needle down through the hole that is diagonal from the one you came up through.

4. Pull the needle up through the back of the fabric again using a hole that has not been used and then down through the hole diagonal from it. Repeat several times until the button is secure.

5. Wrap the thread around itself between the bottom of the button and the fabric three times, double knot the thread, and cut off the remaining thread.

TIGHTEN A SCREW

You might not tighten a screw very often, but it's helpful to know how. Things get loose, and knowledge is power!

1. Look at the screw. It has either a plus or a minus shape on the top. Pick the screwdriver that best fits into the top of the screw: either a flathead screwdriver (with a minus shape at the tip) or a Phillips screwdriver (with a plus shape at the tip).

2. Fit the screwdriver into the top of the screw and turn. Remember righty tighty and lefty loosey: Turn the screwdriver to the right (clockwise) to tighten the screw, and to the left to loosen (or remove) the screw.

3. When the screw is flush against (lined up with) the fixture, it's secure.

CHANGE BATTERIES

Batteries come in different sizes, such as AAA, AA, C, D, and 9-volt. AAA is the smallest and used for smaller, low-powered devices like remotes, and D batteries are bigger and used for larger devices requiring more power, like lanterns. The rectangular 9-volt batteries are often used in smoke detectors.

1. If you're replacing the batteries, open the battery hatch on the device. Look at the battery inside the device and get the same kind. If it's a new device, the directions will tell you what size is needed.

2. If you're replacing batteries, remove the old ones from the device.

3. Batteries have a positive side and a negative side (the flat side). Match the plus and minus signs on the device with the positive and negative ends of the battery.

4. Sometimes there's a spring where you put the batteries. Match the negative end of the battery with the spring and put that end in first. When several batteries are needed, they alternate direction.

5. Close the battery hatch and test the device.

Ask an adult about battery disposal. Some communities recycle them.

SMOKE DETECTORS: WHAT'S THAT BEEP TELLING ME?

If your smoke alarm is beeping every 30 to 60 seconds, it means the device needs a new battery. If this happens, the sound of the alarm is irritating, but you are not in immediate danger. If the sound makes you feel anxious, that is normal and human. Continue to take deep breaths. On the device is a button that allows you to test or hush the device. Press the button to hush it and tell an adult. A loud, continuous beep from your smoke alarm means that your device has detected smoke or a fire. If that happens, quickly alert an adult, have everyone go outside immediately, and call 911.

CHAPTER 2
RINSE AND REPEAT

- SORT CLOTHES

- WASH CLOTHES

- REMOVE LAUNDRY STAINS

- DRY CLOTHES

- IRON CLOTHES

- FOLD LAUNDRY

- CLEAN SHOES/ WASH SNEAKERS

- WASH AND PUT AWAY DISHES

- SWEEP, SWIFFER, MOP

- VACUUM

- DUST

- TAKE OUT THE TRASH

- CLEAN THE BATHROOM SINK AND MIRROR

- CLEAN THE SHOWER AND TUB

- CLEAN THE TOILET

- USE A PLUNGER

SORT CLOTHES

Keeping your clothing clean is an important sign of independence. Learn how to prep your clothes before washing them so you can keep your favorites looking like new for a long time!

- **Sort by color and weight.** Separate dark and light clothing, and heavy clothes from lightweight, to wash separately. Dyes from dark clothing can make your whites less sparkly, and heavy clothes like sweatshirts can leave T-shirts wrinkly. Also, wash bright-colored clothes together. This keeps colors vibrant. If a color bleeds during the wash, don't panic—but don't put the item in the dryer. The heat will set the stain. Just wash it again.

- **Read the labels.** Check the labels on the inside of your clothing. They will tell you how to wash the item. You may learn that your favorite outfit can't go in the dryer (it'll shrink!) or needs dry cleaning.

- **Check your pockets.** Empty your pockets! Things like tissues, gum, and paper can get goopy during the wash and stick to the fabric of your clothing. Items such as pens and makeup can leave stains.

- **Get ahead of stains.** Before washing them, look over your clothes for stains that can be pretreated. See "Remove laundry stains" on page 26 for more information.

ECO-TIPS:

- Go green while getting clean! Wash clothing in cold water. It saves energy and gets clothing just as clean as hot water.

- Look for detergents sold in boxes and avoid plastic jugs when possible. It's a small change that helps the planet.

WASH CLOTHES

Once you learn how to wash your own clothes, you'll never have to ask, "Is my favorite shirt washed yet?" You'll be in charge of your clothes, from hamper to washer to dryer, back to you!

TO MACHINE-WASH

1. Ask an adult about the different settings. Most machines have options for the size of the load you're washing, speed (ranging from delicate to heavy), and water temperature (cold is gentler and saves energy; warm or hot is good for dirtier items).

2. Select the appropriate load size, washing cycle, and temperature.

3. Add detergent to the dispenser or the laundry drum (where the laundry goes). Read the container for how much to add—you can also check with an adult. Never put pods in the dispenser; they go into the drum. If you use liquid fabric softener, add it to the dispenser or drum before the start of the cycle or before the final rinse of the wash cycle.

4. Load sorted clothing into the machine, making sure clothes aren't folded or wadded together.

5. Press Start.

TO HAND-WASH

1. Once in a while, a clothing label will suggest hand-washing. Or maybe you're on vacation and need to clean undergarments or something that's stained. To start, fill the sink with water. Add a tiny amount of detergent. Dab a bit of detergent on any stains and scrub with a washcloth.

2. Put the item in the water. Use your hands to swish the clothing around.

3. Let the item soak for a few minutes. Take it out and squeeze gently.

4. Refill the sink with fresh water, and dunk and swirl the garment again. Rinse and repeat this step until the garment is soap-free.

5. Gently squeeze out any water and lay the garment on a dry towel. Roll up the towel, squeezing and pushing out water as you roll. Shake the garment gently and hang or lay it flat on another dry towel to fully dry.

CAN I WEAR THESE AGAIN?

Jean experts recommend washing your jeans after three to ten wears, so it's okay if you choose to wear them more than once between washes. Of course, if you notice a stain or they smell, definitely wash them no matter how many hours (or minutes!) you've been wearing them.

REMOVE LAUNDRY STAINS

Washing stained clothing might result in making the stain permanent, so take some quick action to prevent ruining your favorite stuff. The faster you can clean a stain, the more likely you'll be to erase its existence!

1. **Pretreat.** Pretreat pesky stains before tossing clothing into the machine. Squirt stain remover or dab a bit of detergent on the stain and let it sit for a few minutes. It's like giving the stains a "time-out" before washing them away.

2. **Soak and scrub.** Tougher stains, like blood, require a little more effort. After pretreating the stained garment, let it soak in cold water for a few minutes. Then gently rub the stain between the fabric. You could even grab an old toothbrush and softly scrub.

3. **Wash.** Once the stain is out, wash as normal. If a stain remains, repeat the process. Heat will set a stain, so don't dry the item of clothing until you're satisfied the stain has been removed.

DRY CLOTHES

Selecting the correct dryer cycle preserves the life of your clothes. Over-drying can shrink, fade, and break down clothing fibers. Cycles may include:

- **Regular:** Save this hot setting for heavy items like towels, bulky sweatshirts, and jeans.

- **Permanent press:** This setting is your best friend. Great for drying and preserving most clothes.

- **Delicate:** For stretchy clothing like leggings, sports bras, and anything with elastic. The delicate cycle also combats smells, so it's great for drying anything sweaty.

- **Tumble dry:** The slowest, gentlest cycle, good for special clothing that might shrink or has decorative items, such as beading or sequins—turn those inside out before drying.

LINE-DRYING

Hang clothing outside or drape it over deck railings or outdoor furniture. You can also line-dry clothing inside on a drying rack.

DRY IN A DRYER

1. Clean out the lint trap before each load. Ask an adult where the lint trap is located on your dryer. Keeping the lint trap clean will help the dryer work more efficiently and prevent fires.

2. Move clothing from the washing machine to the dryer, untangling garments along the way. Take out clothes that don't go in the dryer. Inspect for any stains. Re-treat any stained items (see previous page) and rewash.

3. Select your cycle and press Start.

IRON CLOTHES

Your favorite shirt just came out of the dryer, *wrinkled*! Don't despair—pressing it with an iron will fix that. Check with a caregiver before using an iron, as it gets extremely hot and must be handled with care.

DON'T IRON:

- Velvet
- Anything with sequins
- Fabrics marked "wrinkle-resistant" (such as high-performance sports clothing)
- Corduroy

IRON INSIDE OUT:

- Rayon, linen, and satin items
- Items with iron-ons or rubber/plastic embellishments

SUPPLIES NEEDED:

- Ironing board
- Iron
- Water (optional)

1. Check the tags on your piece of clothing to make sure it can be ironed.

2. Unfold the ironing board in a safe place (away from small children and pets) near an electrical outlet.

3. Look at the iron's temperature options and choose the desired setting. To use the optional steam function (that helps further remove wrinkles), fill the little hole in the iron with water.

4. Plug in the iron and place it on the ironing board with the pointy tip of the iron facing up. Wait a few minutes for the iron to heat up. Some irons beep when they are ready to use.

5. Spread the article of clothing over the ironing board in a single layer and straighten it to lie flat. Holding the handle, gently move the iron over the item in a back-and-forth motion. If using steam, point the iron away from you and push the button to make steam, then slide the iron over the wrinkled area. Reposition the item and repeat until the entire item is ironed.

6. Fold any creases, pleats, or seams as you iron. Unfold collars and turn buttoned items inside out to iron them. Iron anything with ruffles inside out.

7. Turn off and unplug the iron, placing it upright. Don't leave the iron unattended until it's cool.

Accidents can happen. If you get burned, run the burn under cool water for about 20 minutes. Let an adult know immediately. Never apply ice or freezing cold water to a burn.

FOLD LAUNDRY

Congratulations: This is the final stage of your laundry's journey from hamper to drawer!

1. Start with a flat surface, like a table or bed. Lay the article of clothing flat on the surface, smoothing it free of wrinkles.

2. For a shirt or sweater, begin with the sleeves. Fold them inward, toward the center, so that the shirt is divided into thirds. After that, fold the top half over the bottom half.

3. Fold pants in half lengthwise by placing one pant leg over the other and smoothing. Next, fold the pants in half up from the bottom so the bottom hem of the pant leg touches the waistband. (Jeans can be folded into thirds— they don't wrinkle as easily as other pants.)

4. Place freshly folded clothing into your drawers or hang pants in your closet.

Some clothes stay nicer on a hanger in a closet, including dresses, button-up shirts, and flowy skirts. No need to fold these—hang 'em instead!

CLEAN SHOES/ WASH SNEAKERS

Sneakers looking a little grubby? Don't despair! Bring your shoes back to life with a few simple steps that'll put the pep back in your step.

SUPPLIES NEEDED:

- Soft scrub brush or cloth
- Liquid laundry detergent

1. Use a damp cloth or soft scrub brush to wipe off as much grime as possible from the shoe. (If the shoes are leather, use a dry, soft brush to wipe, and don't machine-wash. Leather and water don't mix!)

2. Leather shoes cannot go in the washing machine, but canvas shoes can—check with an adult to make sure they're okay to wash. Remove the laces and insoles (the inner foot pads).

3. Set the temperature to cold and wash sneakers with something sturdy, like towels, to protect your sneakers from getting banged up.

4. Instead of using the dryer (this can damage sneakers), find a well-ventilated area for your sneakers to dry naturally, such as near a window or fan, or outside in the sunshine.

If you happen to step in dog poop, don't machine-wash your shoes. Instead, hose off the soles outside and use a stick or disposable utensil to scrape the poop out of the crevices. Let them dry outside.

WASH AND PUT AWAY DISHES

Everyone loves mealtime. But every meal comes with prep and cleanup. Helping wash and put away dishes is a thoughtful way to show appreciation for the person who prepared the meal.

TO HAND-WASH DISHES

Keep these items out of the dishwasher:

- Anything made of wood, like cutting boards and wooden spoons
- Nonstick cookware, such as baking sheets, pots, and pans
- Fine china or hand-painted dishes
- Cheese graters and sharp carving knives (they can get dull)
- Some soft plastics (check the label to learn if they are top rack dishwasher-safe)

1. Scrape food off plates and into the garbage can or disposal. Don't pour the grease from pans down the sink drain; just sop up the grease with a paper towel and toss.

2. Fill the sink or a large container with hot, soapy water.

3. Stack dishes and bowls in the water to soak for a bit. Give utensils their own bubble bath in a bowl of soapy water.

4. Use a clean, soapy sponge to scrub the top and bottom of each item. Work from the least dirty to the dirtiest item.

5. Run fresh water over each item until all food, residue, and soap suds are gone.

6. Either towel-dry each item, or stack them in a drying rack.

TO MACHINE-WASH DISHES

1. Scrape dishes clean and pre-rinse them to remove excess residue.

2. Place plates and bowls into the slots in the lower level, facing in the same direction.

3. Place cups, glasses, and any "top-rack-only" items upside down in the top level.

4. Load the utensils into the designated basket. Point forks and knives downward so the person removing them doesn't get poked.

5. Add detergent to the detergent compartment. Shut the compartment and the dishwasher door. Lock the dishwasher door.

6. Select the correct cycle (most dishes can be washed on a regular cycle), and press Start.

SWEEP, SWIFFER, MOP

Walking on a dirty floor feels yucky. It's easy to clean, so why not learn?

SWEEP

1. Remove clutter from the area.

2. Grab a broom and dustpan. Starting in a corner, pull the broom toward you in small strokes. Move the debris and dust into a pile in the center. Work your way around the room this way.

3. Sweep the pile into the dustpan. Empty the dustpan in the garbage.

4. Clean the broom of any dust or debris by knocking it against a hard surface outside.

SWIFFER

A Swiffer is a combination sweeper/mop that's great for a quick daily cleaning. Use dry pads to clean dirt, dust, hair, or lint and wet pads for spills or sticky areas.

1. Attach a fresh Swiffer cloth.

2. Push the Swiffer back and forth across the area you want to clean. Discard and replace the cloth when it gets dirty.

MOP

1. Sweep your floor to pick up excess debris.

2. Add cleaning detergent to a bucket (read the directions for the right amount), then fill the bucket with hot water.

3. Dip the mop in the bucket and wring it out until it's damp, not soaking wet.

4. Working from one end of the room, drag the mop across the floor, pressing down slightly. Move backward so you are always walking on a dry part of the floor.

5. Dip the mop in the bucket and wring often.

6. Empty and refill the bucket if it gets dirty.

7. Rinse the soapy mop well. Rinse and fill the bucket with just hot water and use the mop to rinse the floor.

Note: Some people choose to get down on their hands and knees to scrub their floors. Do what works best for you and your family.

VACUUM

Vacuuming is like a magic process that removes dirt, dust, hair, and pet dander (if you have a pet). It also protects your carpet or rug so it will last longer.

1. Put on shoes to protect your feet and pick up clutter in the area.

2. Plug in your vacuum and adjust the vacuum height for the carpet or bare floor—an adult can show you where this setting is located, if needed.

3. Starting at the edge of the carpet, slowly move the vacuum forward a few feet and then backward.

4. Shift the direction slightly and push forward again, this time right next to where you just cleaned. With thicker carpets, you may notice lines in the carpet where you vacuumed.

5. Repeat pushing the vacuum forward and backward, shifting over slightly each time, until you have covered the whole carpet.

6. If needed, use the attachments (like the hose) to clean tight spots like corners, stairs, and under furniture.

7. Unplug the vacuum. Empty the bag or canister carefully in the trash so that your vacuum is clean and ready to go. Secure the cord and put the vacuum away.

DUST

When you dust, you get rid of dust, pollen, and germs, as well as any pet fur or dander that may be present. This can have a positive impact on your health and the health of your family members and guests in your home—especially people with allergies. And it's so easy to do!

1. Declutter. Move items off of shelves and furniture.

2. Fold a cloth (microfiber if possible) in half. Use one side of the cloth and when it gets dirty, switch to the other side.

3. Starting at the highest point in the room, dust hard surfaces by sliding the cloth across them. Work your way down to lower surfaces and make sure to get in corners and crevices. Clean off tables, bookshelves, window blinds, lamps, and anything else that collects dust.

4. Dust the items you removed from the shelves and furniture and replace them.

5. Rinse off and wring out the cloth and place it in the laundry hamper.

Should you use a dry cloth or wet cloth? A dry cloth cleans without damaging the furniture. But some experts say to use a damp cloth, especially for very dirty surfaces. Check with an adult first—a cloth that's too wet can cause water stains on unsealed wood furniture and ruin electronics.

TAKE OUT THE TRASH

Taking out the trash is an important job. Think about it—removing the trash from your home helps you and your family maintain a clean, safe, and nice-smelling environment. And recycling is even more important—you're preparing used packaging to have a new life, which helps your world!

DISPOSE OF GARBAGE

1. Empty bathroom and bedroom garbage cans into the kitchen can (lined with a garbage bag) so you can take out one big bag.

2. Tie the kitchen trash bag securely and remove it from the can.

3. Put the bag in an outdoor garbage can or wherever you take your trash. Make sure the garbage can lid is sealed.

4. Put a new trash bag in your kitchen garbage can.

RECYCLE

1. Make sure all food is removed from containers.

2. Clean containers with water and dry them if needed.

3. Break down cardboard boxes at the creases and flatten them.

4. Separate recyclable items and place them in the correct bins. For example, some communities ask you to put cardboard and paper into one bin and plastics into another bin. Different communities have different rules, so ask an adult for guidance on the rules for your area.

CLEAN THE BATHROOM SINK AND MIRROR

Bathroom sinks get dirty, between all the tooth-brushing and hand-washing that takes place there. Cleaning the sink and mirror regularly helps keep them sparkling and germ-free.

SINK

1. Remove all items from the countertop.

2. Spray the sink basin and drain with an all-purpose cleaner and let it sit for a few minutes. Wipe with a damp cloth or sponge or cleaning wipe. Rinse well with warm water.

3. Mix a little dish soap and water on a cloth or sponge (or use a wipe) and clean the faucet. Use an old toothbrush to scrub stains or hard-to-reach areas. Rinse with warm water. Dry the faucet with a dry cloth. Repeat for the countertop.

4. Put everything back on the countertop.

MIRROR

1. Spray glass cleaner onto a microfiber cloth or balled-up newspaper. (Don't spray cleaner directly onto the mirror.)

2. Start cleaning at the top of the mirror. Wipe from side to side as you move down the mirror.

3. When the section of cloth you're using becomes dirty, use a different section until the job is done.

CLEAN THE SHOWER AND TUB

Are you taking more frequent showers and following a daily skin care routine? These are good ways to care for your changing body. Think of cleaning your shower and tub as a gift to yourself: creating a space that makes you feel good.

1. Remove all items like shampoo from the area and wipe down all bottles (especially the bottoms).

2. Spray the shower or tub area, including faucets, with an all-purpose cleaner. Let it sit for three to five minutes. Using a sponge or a mesh scrubber, wipe from the top of the area to the bottom.

3. If you have a shower door, clean that along with the shower area.

4. If you have a shower curtain, mix 1/4 cup of white vinegar with 1 cup of water in a spray bottle. Spray the entire shower curtain with the mixture. If you don't have a spray bottle, use a cloth to wipe the mixture on the curtain.

5. Rinse the entire area thoroughly.

6. Return all items to where they belong.

CLEAN THE TOILET

Nobody loves cleaning a toilet! But the best strategy is to clean your toilet regularly. The more frequently you clean it, the easier the job is each time. Use new wipes and clean sponges or cloths for each part of the toilet.

1. Put on rubber gloves if you have them. Pour toilet cleaner in the bowl. Let it sit for five minutes.

2. Use a toilet brush to scrub the bowl and underneath the rim. Flush. Replace the brush in its holder.

3. Spray and wipe the top of the tank and the flush handle (or use a cleaning wipe).

4. Spray and wipe the outside and inside of the lid.

5. Spray and wipe the top, then bottom, of the toilet seat, then the toilet bowl rim.

6. Clean the small area between the toilet seat and the tank.

7. Spray and wipe the outside of the toilet bowl and the surrounding floor.

8. When you are finished, rinse out any sponges and wash any cloths. Toss all used wipes.

USE A PLUNGER

Sometimes when a toilet won't flush (or the water starts rising!), you need to use a plunger. Don't panic—this is easier than it sounds.

1. Place the rubber part of the plunger over the opening at the bottom of the toilet. Make sure the hole is completely covered.

2. Hold on to the handle and push up and down for 20 seconds or so.

3. Lift the plunger up for the water to drain.

4. If it doesn't work the first time, you can try again. You may need to have an adult call a plumber if the clog doesn't move.

CHAPTER 3
COOKING UP KNOWLEDGE

- USE KITCHEN TOOLS

- USE KITCHEN APPLIANCES

- PUT OUT A KITCHEN FIRE

- CUT AN ONION

- BOIL PASTA

USE KITCHEN TOOLS

It's easy to be overwhelmed by fancy kitchen gadgets. But all you need to whip up something scrumptious is a few basic tools. Let's explore some of them:

- **Pots:** Deep cooking vessels with tall sides and two handles, used to simmer or boil liquids.
- **Pans**: Shallower containers with one handle, perfect for making sauces, reheating soups, or boiling small quantities of water.
- **Skillet/frying pan:** These pans typically have sloped sides and are used to fry, sauté, or make eggs.
- **Baking sheets:** Great for roasting vegetables . . . or baking cookies! They are flat, rimmed sheets.

CHEF'S KNIFE

Its long, thin, non-serrated (no teeth) blade is handy for cutting ingredients on a cutting board. Get permission before using it.

1. Firmly grip the knife in your dominant hand and point it away from yourself and others.

2. With your other hand, carefully hold the ingredient to be sliced.

3. Press the knife into the food and cut with a back-and-forth motion.

CUTTING BOARD

Protect your countertops and your fingers by always slicing bread, veggies, and meat on a cutting board. If you're able, use separate cutting boards for meat and veggies. Cutting boards come in plastic and wood; both are fine to use for any ingredient. Wash both types with soap and warm water, and never put wood or plastic into the dishwasher.

MANUAL CAN OPENER

1. Open the handles of the can opener and clamp the can's lid between the sharp cutting wheel and the notched wheel.

2. Squeeze the two handles together until you feel the cutting wheel puncture the can.

3. Twist the knob away from you, making the can rotate and slicing the lid.

4. Keep twisting until the lid separates from the can. Carefully remove the lid.

ELECTRIC CAN OPENER

1. Place the can opener on a stable surface.

2. Line up the can's rim with the cutting wheel.

3. Press down (or press Start) to activate the opener.

4. When it stops, carefully remove the lid.

USE KITCHEN APPLIANCES

Some kitchen appliances might seem intimidating, but in a few steps, you'll learn how to use them to build your cooking and meal prep skills.

MICROWAVE

1. Place food in a microwave-safe dish (labeled on the bottom; glass and ceramic are generally safe). Cover the dish with a paper towel to avoid splattering. Don't microwave aluminum foil, metal, plastic, or Styrofoam.

2. Press Time/Cook and enter the number of minutes or seconds you want to microwave your food. (Some microwaves have pre-selections for food like "popcorn"— pressing this button will automatically start the cooking.)

3. Press Start. Stay in the room while the microwave cooks.

4. Using oven mitts, if necessary, remove the dish from the microwave. Carefully test a bite. Microwaving sometimes heats unevenly, so stir to distribute the heat. And look out: sometimes microwaved food can get very hot!

TOASTER OVEN

Use a toaster oven to cook everything from cookies to tuna melts to nachos.

1. Place food on a baking sheet or toaster rack.

2. Choose the desired temperature, time, and settings (toast vs. cook). Press Start. Stay nearby as the food cooks.

3. Use oven mitts to remove cooked food onto a heat-safe surface.

TOASTER

1. Pop the item (bread, bagel, waffle) into the slot.

2. Adjust the settings knob. For darker toast, turn the knob to the right.

3. Push down the springy lever and stick around until it pops up.

4. Use fingers (not a utensil) to remove the toasted item.

BLENDER

1. Plug in the blender.

2. Add the ingredients, then secure the lid.

3. Press the Start button and select the desired setting.

4. Blend until you have your desired consistency.

5. Turn off and unplug the blender and pour your drink into a glass.

6. Rinse all parts of the blender, being particularly careful with the blade. You can hand-wash the container or put it in the dishwasher.

PREHEATING AN OVEN: WHY AND HOW?

Recipes often instruct you to preheat so the oven is at the right temperature when you're ready to cook your food. Otherwise your food might not cook thoroughly, and might even look bad (picture flat cookies)!

1. Turn on the oven. All ovens are different, so ask an adult if you are unsure how.

2. Turn the temperature dial or punch in the numbers to the desired temperature.

3. Wait for a beep or light to indicate that the desired temperature has been reached. This usually takes 10 minutes or less. Keep an eye on the clock for an oven that doesn't beep.

4. Put the item in the oven, carefully but quickly, so too much heat doesn't escape.

Convection ovens cook faster, so you can either reduce your cooking temperature by 25 degrees or your cook time by 25 percent. Some convection ovens have an auto-adjustment feature, which will do the math for you. Ask an adult if your oven has this feature.

PUT OUT A KITCHEN FIRE

If a fire erupts, call an adult. Make sure your family keeps a fire extinguisher in the kitchen for emergencies. (Everyone should practice using it.) Your adult may decide the fire requires the fire department, so one of you may call 911. Once you've called 911, go outside, away from the fire.

OVEN FIRE

Don't open the oven door. This will add oxygen and enlarge the fire. Keep the door closed and the fire will eventually burn itself out.

STOVETOP FIRE

This type of fire is more dangerous. Snuff out flames by smothering a small fire with a pot lid or cookie sheet. This cuts the oxygen supply. If the fire continues, smother it with baking soda or blast it with the fire extinguisher.

Don't throw water on a kitchen fire! Most kitchen fires are from grease. Pouring water onto a grease fire can make the hot grease splatter and can make the fire worse.

CUT AN ONION

Place the onion in the freezer for 20 minutes before cutting it or wear goggles if you don't want your eyes to tear while you're cutting.

1. Place the onion on a cutting board. Use a sharp knife to carefully cut the onion in half. Ask an adult for help, if needed.

2. Cut off the ends of the onion, remove the skins, and throw them away.

3. Lay half of the onion cut-side down on the cutting board. Cut lengthwise from root to stem. Repeat with the other half of the onion.

4. Holding the onion firmly, with your fingers carefully out of the way of the knife, cut the onion into the size the recipe requests. To mince the onion, cut slices and then cut again so that the pieces are shaped like little squares. Watch your fingertips and knuckles!

5. Wash your hands.

BOIL PASTA

Once you can make pasta, you're officially a cook! Learning this skill also opens the door to boiling chicken, potatoes, grains, and veggies.

1. Fill a large cooking pot halfway with water and put it on the stove.

2. Turn the heat on the stove to high. You may want to ask an adult for help.

3. Put the lid on and wait for the water to boil. (Covering the water makes it boil faster.) Bubbles rise to the top when the water is boiling.

4. Add a pinch of salt if desired so the pasta doesn't stick together and for flavor.

5. Once the water is boiling, add the pasta and stir, making sure it's all submerged. Stir occasionally to prevent sticking.

6. Cook according to package directions (most pastas cook in 8 to 12 minutes). Place a colander in the sink. Set a timer to alert you when the pasta is done cooking.

7. When the timer sounds, use tongs to take out a piece of pasta, rinse it under cold water, and taste it. If the pasta is soft but not crunchy, it's ready.

8. Turn off the stovetop. Wearing oven mitts, carefully carry the pot to the sink and slowly pour the pasta away from you (to avoid steam in your face) into the colander. Shake the colander to drain the water. Let an adult help if needed.

9. Rinse the pasta or toss with a little olive oil (or whatever your family does). Enjoy!

CHAPTER 4
SOUND BODY, SOUND MIND

- SLEEP TIGHT

- MOVE YOUR BODY

- EAT RIGHT

- ADOPT HEALTHY HABITS

- PRACTICE FIRST AID

- VISIT THE DOCTOR

- VISIT THE DENTIST/ORTHODONTIST

- COPE WITH STRESS

- UNDERSTAND YOUR EMOTIONS

- THINK AND RESPOND

SLEEP TIGHT

Think about sleep as the glue that holds you together! Our bodies need deep, regular sleep to stay healthy, balance emotions, think clearly, and manage stress. If you prioritize sleep, you'll quickly notice positive differences in how you feel.

USE THESE STEPS TO DEVELOP STRONG SLEEP SKILLS:

- **Establish a relaxing routine.** A regular routine sends signals to your body that it's time to wind down. Figure out what works for you. You might:
  - Take a warm shower.
  - Stretch and meditate.
  - Dim the lights.
  - Read or journal in bed.
  - Listen to quiet music.

- **Develop a rhythm.** Go to bed and wake up at consistent times—even on weekends! This establishes patterns in your body so you more naturally fall asleep and wake up rested.

- **Create your own sleep haven.** Make your bedroom into a zen den with comfortable bedding, shades, and a fan or sound machine if you wish.

- **Put your screen to bed, too.** Stay off your screens for at least an hour before bed. The light from these screens interferes with sleep hormone production.

- **Steer clear of stimulants.** Keep away from caffeine and sugar, especially in the evening. These substances fight your body's ability to fall asleep and stay asleep.

MOVE YOUR BODY

Moving your body is essential to staying physically and emotionally fit. Daily exercise keeps our bodies strong, helps with sleep, and reduces stress. Here's how to get moving:

- **Find activities you enjoy.** Whether it's dancing in your living room, swimming, playing a sport, or walking your dog, choose movement that makes you happy. When exercise is fun, you stay motivated to keep doing it.

- **Mix it up.** Surprise your muscles and stay engaged by changing up your routine. Do an online yoga session one day; go for a bike ride the next.

- **Aim for aerobics.** Try some activities that get your heart rate pumping and increase your breathing rate. You can tell that you're at a good level if you can talk during exercise but it's harder than normal.

- **Stay consistent.** Make exercise a daily promise to yourself. Half an hour each day is ideal, but even 10 minutes of movement is better than nothing!

- **Be accountable.** Write down your goals or track your progress on a calendar. Find a buddy or join a class to keep yourself accountable and motivated.

BRAS: THEY'RE HERE TO SUPPORT YOU!

Bras are meant to be supportive and comfortable, no matter what you're doing. The cups should fit and form to the shape of your breast. The cups shouldn't be too big, nor should your breasts overflow outside the cups. The straps should feel good, not dig into your skin or leave a mark. The band in the middle of your back should stay where it is and not ride up. A good fit means you can slide two fingers under the band comfortably and wear the bra on its loosest setting when it is new. A salesperson can measure you for the right fit.

EAT RIGHT

Food can be fun! With so many options, we could literally eat something different every day. But we all have our favorites. The important thing to remember is balance. Eating right is all about nourishing your growing body with a well-balanced diet that includes a variety of food. Here's how:

- **Eat the rainbow.** Red grapes, blueberries, orange carrots, green cucumbers: Every color comes with its own nutritional power. So mix it up with a wide range of colors.

- **Choose whole grains.** Whole-grain breads and cereals are high in fiber, vitamins, and minerals that promote good digestion and heart health.

- **Go whole.** The best foods for us are the ones that look like nature made them. For example, a potato has more value than a potato chip or French fry. Try to include lots of whole foods in your day.

- **Respect limits.** Sugary and processed foods (like those that come in a colorful package) can be hard to resist. Sadly, they offer nothing helpful to your body. And did you know, the more of these you eat, the more you crave them? Likewise, the less of these you eat, the less you crave them. Set limits for yourself and look for less processed foods that offer the sweetness or saltiness you crave.

- **Embrace your inner foodie.** We all have foods we love, but our taste buds are always changing. Challenge yourself to expand your culinary palate. Try some new foods. Go food shopping with your caregiver and look for interesting foods to buy. Find new recipes. Cook with a friend!

- **Choose lean proteins and healthy fats.** These help maintain strong energy and alertness. Chicken, fish, and beans are lean proteins that help with muscle growth and repair. Healthy fats found in foods like avocados and nuts support brain health.

ADOPT HEALTHY HABITS

Do you have trouble getting out of bed in the morning? Or staying motivated in school? Or even just feeling upbeat and happy? If so, picking up a few healthy habits can change your energy and outlook!

RISE AND DINE

Kickstart your day with a breakfast that packs a punch. A mix of whole grains, fruit, and protein will keep you energized through the morning. If breakfast isn't your thing, try something small but powerful like a breakfast drink, smoothie, or hard-boiled egg.

THE GREAT OUTDOORS

Spending time in nature boosts your mood and reduces stress. Spend at least 10 minutes each day outside, taking a walk, eating lunch under a tree, riding your bike after dinner—whatever you like.

POSITIVE POWER

Each day, take a few minutes to practice feeling gratitude. What are you thankful for? Challenge negative thoughts with positive ones. How can you think about something differently? Your mindset has the power to transform your entire outlook.

SUDS AND SCRUBS

Be a total hand-washer. Wash your hands regularly and after using the bathroom, before eating, and after being in public places. Hand-washing is one of the best defenses against getting sick.

HYDRATION CELEBRATION

Keep water with you at all times. Staying hydrated is great for your skin! It also improves brain function, speeds digestion, boosts energy, and more. Aim to drink at least eight cups, or 64 ounces, of water each day.

SNOOZE AND SHINE

Is your sleep schedule a little sketchy? Power up with quality snooze time. At your age, at least 8 to 10 hours a night is needed to recharge your body, boost brainpower, and repair muscles. See page 53 for more sleep strategies.

EXERCISE

Move your body every day. Exercise is totally linked to how you feel. See page 54 for ideas.

PRACTICE FIRST AID

It can be scary when someone gets hurt, but it's much less scary if you know what to do. Always tell an adult, too.

BURNS

- Run the burn under cool water or apply a cool, wet washcloth.

- Avoid extreme cold and never ice a burn.

- Call a doctor if the burn continues to be painful or begins to blister, swell, or the skin changes color.

SPLINTERS

1. Clean the area around the splinter with soap and water.

2. Wash your hands and sterilize tweezers with rubbing alcohol.

3. If the splinter is partly exposed, use tweezers to gently pull out the splinter in the same direction it's going.

4. For a deeper splinter, soaking the area in warm water for about 15 minutes may soften the skin, making it easier to access the splinter.

5. Wash the area again with soapy water.

6. For more severe splinters that won't come out, see an adult.

SCRAPES AND CUTS

1. Stop any bleeding by applying pressure with a towel or cloth against the wound.

2. Wash the area with soap and water.

3. Apply antibiotic cream and cover the cut with a bandage.

4. See an adult if the wound is deeper than ¼ inch or longer than ½ inch.

NOSEBLEEDS

1. Tilt your head forward.

2. With a tissue, pinch the soft part of your nostrils together. Hold for at least 10 minutes.

3. If possible, apply a cold pack to your nose or back of your neck.

4. Tell a trusted adult if the bleeding continues for more than 20 minutes.

BEE STINGS

1. Use your fingers or tweezers to gently remove the stinger.

2. Wash the area with soap and water.

3. Apply a cold pack to reduce swelling.

4. If the site remains painful, ask an adult for an over-the-counter pain reliever.

5. If you experience any signs of allergic reaction, such as hives, swelling, nausea, dizziness, or difficulty breathing, get help immediately.

MAKE YOUR OWN FIRST AID KIT

It's a good idea to have a first aid kit handy in your house, and to bring one when traveling. You never know what could happen, and it's smart to be prepared!

Find a small container; a plastic bin with a lid works well. Fill the inside of the container with the following items:

- Bandages and gauze of different sizes
- Adhesive tape
- Antiseptic wipes or cream
- Tweezers
- Disposable gloves
- Cotton balls and swabs
- Hydrogen peroxide or isopropyl alcohol (rubbing alcohol) for disinfecting
- Thermometer
- Pain reliever (like Tylenol or Advil)
- Antihistamines for allergic reactions (like Benadryl)
- Heat and cold packs
- Scissors

Also, make a list of emergency contacts and phone numbers (like doctors and poison control) and post it where everyone in your family can find it.

VISIT THE DOCTOR

Visiting the doctor is important to your health and well-being. Don't be afraid to ask questions and be honest. If you don't feel comfortable talking with your doctor, tell your caregiver so they can speak on your behalf.

- **What happens:** During your annual checkup, your doctor assesses your overall health to make sure you're meeting developmental and growth milestones. This includes measuring your height, weight, and blood pressure, screening your hearing and vision, and examining your body. You might get an immunization as well. The doctor might ask about your family history and daily habits.

- **Questions and concerns:** This is your chance to ask about things you might be wondering about. Bring a list of questions, such as "When will I get my period, and how will I know it's coming?" And remember that even if you feel uncomfortable talking about personal stuff, your doctor has heard it all before and is there to help.

- **Privacy:** During adolescence, doctors often examine patients without their parents present, especially when examining your reproductive parts. Tell the doctor what makes you comfortable, such as having another person present. Although doctors work with your parents and are required to speak up if they feel you are in danger of harm, they aren't required to share everything you tell them. If you want to keep your discussion confidential, tell your doctor.

VISIT THE DENTIST/ ORTHODONTIST

The dentist and orthodontist are responsible for the health of your teeth and gums. You can help by brushing and flossing regularly and visiting the dentist twice a year.

THE DENTIST

Just like with the doctor, visiting the dentist is essential for your health and well-being. Here, too, ask questions and be honest. The dentist is there to help you.

- **Cavities.** Sometimes a dentist finds a cavity, or a tiny hole in your teeth, caused by bacteria, frequent snacking, sugary drinks, or not cleaning your teeth well. Dentists treat cavities to prevent infection and tooth loss.

- **X-rays.** Dentists sometimes take x-rays of your teeth and jaw. This helps them determine what's going on under your gums and what care you need to prevent health issues.

- **Deep cleaning.** Hygienists use a tool called a scaler to remove plaque between your teeth and around your gums, followed by a cleaning with a high-powered toothbrush and special toothpaste. Then they floss your teeth and apply a fluoride treatment to your teeth to prevent cavities.

THE ORTHODONTIST

The goal of an orthodontist is to align your teeth, whether to prevent dental issues like gum disease or to enhance your smile. They can determine if you need braces, a palate expander (that creates more space in your mouth by widening your jaw), or a retainer. All of these devices help align your teeth to prevent oral health care issues and lead to greater health and well-being.

COPE WITH STRESS

Do you get stressed often? If so, you are not alone! Feeling stressed or anxious is part of being human. We all feel stress and anxiety—even adults. And we feel these things at different moments, for different reasons. These activities can help reduce stress:

- **Talk to a trusted adult.** They can help you understand your feelings and give you some ideas for how to manage your emotions. This can be hard at first, so try telling them what you need. For example, *"I am struggling with something, and hope you could give me some advice."* Or *"I don't need advice right now; I'm just hoping you can listen."*

- **Mindfulness.** This means focusing on the present moment. Practice being present when doing everyday tasks like brushing your teeth. Focus on the feel of the toothbrush against your gums and smell and taste the mint-flavored toothpaste. Mindfulness becomes easier as you practice it.

- **Meditation.** When people meditate, they often focus on  their breath or on an image, or by repeating a positive statement in their head. This is called a mantra. You can find "free guided meditations" on YouTube for inspiration.

CONTINUED

- **Breathe.** Box breathing is easy, and you can practice anywhere without anyone else knowing! Breathe in for a count of four, hold for four seconds, breathe out for four and hold the breath for four seconds. Repeat until your body feels more relaxed.

- **Exercise.** Say you get in a fight with a friend. You're really stressed! So you decide to take a walk in your neighborhood. When you return home, you realize you've worked off some of that anxious energy. Now you can more clearly think about how to manage the challenge with your friend in a way that fits with your values.

- **Unplug.** Limit screen time to avoid stress from social media and video games. Very often, less is more.

- **Sleep.** Research shows that when you're sleeping, your body and brain are busy recharging. You need this time recharging to learn, grow, perform everyday tasks, and manage emotions like stress and anxiety. Good sleep sets you up for success.

UNDERSTAND YOUR EMOTIONS

When you understand your emotions, you can figure out what they're telling you and how to deal with them.

- Sometimes you might feel mad, sad, disappointed, rejected, or excluded. Other moments you will feel happy, excited, proud, or grateful. Everyone feels excluded or rejected at one point, just as we all feel excited or happy at others.

- We all feel different things at different times and for different reasons. Maybe your friend worries about her math grade, but you worry more about soccer practice. We may worry about different things, but we all worry about something.

- During adolescence it can sometimes feel like you are on a roller coaster of emotions. One minute you're laughing with friends and having an amazing time, and then someone says something that makes you want to cry. Maybe you're feeling angry with your parents and surprised by how angry you are because you can feel it in your whole body. It is normal for emotions to go up and down and be this big during this phase of life. It happens because of the increased level of hormones that are part of growing up.

- When you feel an emotion, see if you can name it. For example, *"I feel frustrated"* or *"I feel stressed."* Say it out loud.

- Now consider why you feel this way. If you feel frustrated, think about the reason. *"I feel frustrated because I don't understand this math problem."* Give yourself credit. You may not get the math problem, but you understand your emotion. That's the first step in solving the problem.

THINK AND RESPOND

You just learned about understanding your emotions. Now you need to figure out how to respond. Let's put this together, starting with an example: A friend has a party. You're not invited. What to do? Pause, take a few deep breaths, and ask yourself:

- *What am I feeling?* Try to identify the feeling and name it. Pick one or a few that you feel best describes how you are feeling. *I am feeling angry, hurt, and disappointed.* Naming a feeling is a strategy that can make you feel better—it'll also help you figure out what you need and how you can express it.

- *What do I need? How can I express this emotion in a way that is beneficial to me and those around me?* Unfortunately, you can't *make* a friend invite you. But if you are angry or hurt, you could tell a sibling or parent how you are feeling. Or find another outlet, like writing in a journal or drawing about how you are feeling. Maybe you prefer to distract yourself by doing something you love to do. You are in charge of how you will deal with the situation.

If you feel the need to express yourself to the person who hurt you, try to express yourself in a way that shows the kind, amazing, awesome person that you are, rather than in a way that makes you feel worse. Use an I-statement, like, *"I feel hurt and upset that I wasn't invited to your party. I thought we were friends."* And hold your head high. You handled that beautifully.

CHAPTER 5
KEEPING IT CLEAN

- SHOWER AND SHAVE

- KEEP BODY ODOR AWAY

- CARE FOR YOUR SKIN

- CARE FOR YOUR HAIR

- CARE FOR YOUR EARS AND NAILS

- PROTECT YOUR TEETH

SHOWER AND SHAVE

Think of showering as time for self-care and relaxation. Before stepping into the shower, check that you have the supplies you need. Soap and washcloth or loofah? Check! Shampoo and conditioner? Double-check! Razor and shaving cream (if you're shaving)? A towel? Now you're ready to go!

In the shower, remember to wash your whole body. Use extra soap on armpits, private areas, and feet, which can get stinky during the day (to keep body odor at bay, as mentioned earlier). For details on washing your hair, see page 74.

If you decide to shave your body hair, you'll need a razor and shaving cream or soap. To shave any body part, first dampen the skin. Dry hair is harder to shave.

- **Legs:** Lather up your leg with shaving cream or soap. Position the razor at the bottom of your leg, near the ankle. Gently glide the razor up your leg in a soft line. Lift the razor, rinse hair from the blade, and repeat the process, starting each time from a new section. Next, move to the knee. Glide the razor up in shorter motions around the kneecap. Then move to the upper leg and thigh and repeat the process if you wish. Some girls prefer to shave just their lower leg—it's a personal decision.

- **Armpits:** Lather up your armpits, one at a time. Stretch your arm high and position the razor at the top of the armpit. Softly move the razor along the armpit from top to bottom, bottom to top, and side to side.

- **Other ways to remove body hair:** There are other ways to remove unwanted body hair if you prefer, such as depilatory creams that you apply, wait, and then wipe away, along with the body hair. Check with an adult first, and read and follow directions carefully to avoid skin irritation or burning.

If you cut yourself shaving, wash the cut and hold a cloth over the cut to stop the bleeding. Once the bleeding has stopped (it can take a few minutes), apply a bandage. If the cut is bleeding a lot or looks serious, let an adult know.

PERIOD TLC (OR HOW DO I CREATE A PERIOD PACK?)

You won't always be able to predict your period. A period pack is your insurance policy—your trusty backup! It will help you be prepared *and* more confident that you have what you need to take care of yourself.

FILL A SMALL BAG OR PURSE WITH:

- 2 pads
- 2 pantyliners
- Tampon (if you use them)
- Over-the-counter pain reliever (with your caregiver's permission)
- Clean underwear
- A small pack of wipes for cleaning your body
- Plastic bag (to hold your stained underwear)

If you have room, add a spare pair of leggings or shorts you can change into if your clothes get stained.

KEEP BODY ODOR AWAY

Body odor doesn't have to happen. A few quick self-care activities in the morning and evening will help you smell clean and feel confident.

1. Shower or bathe daily. Lather up well all over, giving your armpits, private areas, and feet special attention.

2. Use deodorant in the morning before getting dressed. Find a brand you like, whether it's chemical-free, dry, invisible, or environmentally friendly, or has a fragrance you like. Also, there are two types of products to address body odor. Deodorants mask the smell of body odor with another scent. Antiperspirant deodorants also stop perspiration by blocking your sweat pores. Decide which is right for you.

3. Check clothing labels and choose clothes that breathe. Cotton is a great, breathable fabric; so are cotton-polyester blends. But polyester on its own can trap odor, as can nylon, acrylic, and spandex.

4. Keep deodorant at school or in a gym bag in case you get sweaty.

5. Wash your clothes regularly. Some items, like big sweatshirts and sweaters, don't need to be washed every time you wear them. Underwear, socks, sweaty athletic gear, and any shirt worn next to your skin should be washed after each use.

CARE FOR YOUR SKIN

You may have noticed changes in your skin. Some of these changes can be annoying! It's normal for your skin to be oilier. A good skin care routine can help you care for your changing skin. This includes:

- Washing your face twice a day

- Using a cleanser or soap for your skin type

- Massaging your face gently (don't scrub)

- Applying sunblock with an SPF of 15 or higher 30 minutes before you go outside. Use a nickel-sized blob on your face and about 2 tablespoons on your entire exposed body. Reapply sunblock every two hours, or more frequently if you swim or sweat excessively. Remember that people of all skin tones need to use sunblock. You can buy sunblock that doesn't leave a white residue on your skin.

ACNE HAPPENS

Acne occurs when your pores become clogged. This, unfortunately, is normal, too! Acne refers to the zits, pimples, blackheads, or whiteheads that might appear on your skin—usually on your face, but they can also appear on your arms, neck, and back. Acne happens because your body is producing more oils and sweating more. Doctors say to leave pimples alone, since popping them can cause infection or scarring.

HOW TO CONTROL ACNE

Keeping your face and other areas clean can help prevent acne. Following a healthy diet can help too. There are also special cleansers that you can buy with an adult's help. If you are really struggling with acne, ask an adult to take you to a dermatologist. Don't worry alone! Ask for help.

CARE FOR YOUR HAIR

You may have noticed your body is changing. So is your hair. This is normal. Frequent shampooing will keep it looking nice, especially if your hair is oily.

WASHING YOUR HAIR

Your caregiver can help you determine how frequently to wash your hair and what products to use. It depends whether you have straight, wavy, curly, or tightly curled hair, and if it's soft or coarse. Hair type is determined by genetics, and different types of hair require different care. For example, if you have tightly curled hair, your hair is delicate and requires moisture, whereas a person with straight hair might choose to use products that do not add extra oils to their hair.

1. Wet your hair and scalp with water.

2. Put a quarter-sized amount of shampoo in your hand.

3. Rub the shampoo gently into your scalp and hair.

4. Rinse the shampoo out of your hair until the water runs clear.

5. Put a dime-sized amount of conditioner into your hair and focus on massaging the ends of your hair.

6. Thoroughly rinse the conditioner out of your hair.

7. Dry your hair with a towel.

8. Use a brush, pick, hair dryer, or other tools to style your hair. Apply whatever products you like. Many people with curly and textured hair use hair oil before or during brushing. This helps add moisture to their hair and aid detangling.

Some girls cover their hair during sleep with a silk hair cover called a bonnet. This helps protect their hair and prevents break-age and tangling. Although this is most common in communities of color, it is useful for any person with textured or curly hair, of any ethnicity.

After you swim, wash your hair and use a conditioner. If you swim regularly, wear a swim cap to protect your hair.

CARE FOR YOUR EARS AND NAILS

Your ears and nails tell a story about your self-care habits—if you tend to them often, they'll tell a good one!

EAR CARE

Clean your outer ears with a washcloth, and allow water from the shower to run inside your ears. Pat dry with a towel. Don't use cotton swabs inside your ear—they can push ear wax into the ear canal or damage the eardrum.

EAR PIERCINGS

- Leave new piercings in your ears for four to six weeks. If you remove the earrings too soon, the holes might quickly close.

- Clean the sites 2 to 3 times a day using a cotton swab or cotton pad and the cleaning product you may have gotten with your ear piercings. You can also spray the front and back of your ears with a sterile saline or wound wash solution, rinse with warm water, and dry with a clean tissue or paper towel.

- If the area looks red or feels itchy, wash it and apply antibiotic cream. This could be a sign of an infection, so tell an adult.

NAIL CARE

- Always keep your fingernails clean and trimmed.

- Keep a nail brush or nail clipper with a nail cleaner insert handy.

- Use a gentle nail file to shape your nails. This step isn't necessary, and you only need to file your nails if you like the look or if your nail broke and you need to even it out.

NAIL POLISHING

- Choose colors that express your mood and style.

- Apply a clear base coat, then carefully paint on your chosen polish. (Have someone paint for you if it's hard to paint your dominant hand.)

- Let your nails dry completely.

PROTECT YOUR TEETH

Clean teeth equal a beautiful smile, fresh breath, good overall health, and teeth that'll (hopefully!) last a lifetime.

BRUSHING

Brush your teeth twice a day (with either an electric or a manual toothbrush) to remove food and plaque.

1. Put a pea-sized amount of toothpaste on your toothbrush and wet it.

2. Gently move the brush in a circular motion around your mouth for 2 minutes, cleaning all the teeth and gums, between teeth, and where the teeth and gums meet. Brush your tongue and the front and back of your teeth.

3. Spit and then rinse your mouth with water. Next, rinse your toothbrush before placing it back where it belongs. You can also use mouthwash or cavity rinse, which helps freshen breath and prevent cavities and gum disease.

FLOSSING

Floss daily to prevent food and plaque buildup and gum disease. You can use regular floss or a flossing pick.

1. Using the floss dispenser, cut a piece of floss about 12 inches long.

2. Wrap the floss around the pointer finger on your dominant hand and the thumb of your other hand. Or simply hold the ends of the floss with your fingers.

3. Slide the floss gently in between two teeth and move slowly until you reach the gum. Slide the floss against the teeth and gum to clean the area of any food.

4. Repeat between all your teeth.

BRACES

With braces, there are more places for food to hide. A water flosser helps clean food between your teeth and gums by squirting water in your mouth, dislodging food. And flossing with a threader allows you to get past the wire and between teeth. Your orthodontist may recommend a special mouthwash designed for use with braces.

PART TWO
AT SCHOOL

Being successful in school isn't just about getting good grades. Success also means practicing skills that will help you in school and beyond, such as prioritization, time management, organization, and good study habits. School is also a place where you form relationships, navigate conflict, practice listening and communication, and maybe make lifelong friends. Here is step-by-step guidance to help you master these skills so you can approach school ready to handle everything it throws at you.

CHAPTER 6
ORGANIZATION 101

- KEEP A SCHEDULE

- SET UP FOR SCHOOL SUCCESS

- MASTER HOMEWORK

- ASK FOR HELP

- RESOLVE CONFLICTS WITH
  AUTHORITY FIGURES

KEEP A SCHEDULE

Your days are probably filled with tests at school, homework, after-school activities, and plans with friends. Calendars and daily planners are priceless tools to keep track of it all.

PLANNER

Use a daily planner or homework planner to jot down nightly assignments, test dates, and project deadlines. Many teachers use online tools to share this information. But you may not always have access to a device to check assignments, so it's smart to also write everything down on a paper planner or calendar. Plus, you're more likely to remember something if you write it down.

WALL OR DESK CALENDAR

A wall or desk calendar presents the entire month at a glance. These calendars are great for tracking long-term assignments, after-school activities, and upcoming events, like birthdays. Use one to write down your daily activities and deadlines, then cross off the date box at the end of each day. If you have a long-term assignment with a deadline in the future, use the calendar to count backward from the deadline and figure out how many days you have to prepare. Then you can decide what steps to take each day to get ready.

SET UP FOR SCHOOL SUCCESS

Whether you're reading this book in September or January (or somewhere in between), now is the time to learn the skills of prioritizing, following through, and avoiding distractions. These skills will make your life feel more manageable.

PRIORITIZE

Prioritization means tackling the most important tasks first. You may like to finish the easy assignments first or put something off because it feels overwhelming. But it's best to hit the hard stuff while your brain is fresh, then knock out the simpler assignments. Here's how:

1. **Make a "to-do" list.** Write down everything you have to do.

2. **Organize your tasks.** Categorize each task: Urgent, Important, or It Can Wait. Tackle the Urgent items first, then do the Important tasks, and finally, complete the It Can Wait jobs over the weekend or on a night you don't have much going on.

3. **Check 'em off.** Cross off each task or assignment as you complete it. Satisfying!

FOLLOW THROUGH

To motivate yourself to complete your work, set up small rewards for yourself. For example, *After I finish my homework, I'll reward myself with a little screen time or a favorite snack.* Also, tackle small chunks of tasks at a time, so you aren't overwhelmed. For example, *I'll work for 10 minutes, then take a short break.*

AVOID DISTRACTIONS

When you need to focus, put your devices in another room. Even if you turn on "Do Not Disturb," research shows that just having a device next to you distracts the brain.

If you catch your attention drifting at home or in school, try these strategies:

- **Take a few deep breaths.** Bringing more oxygen into your brain calms your nervous system and refreshes your body.

- **Take a quick break.** Get a drink of water or move your body by walking to the bathroom or into the hallway.

- **Write down your task.** Jot down what you need to accomplish. It will remind you of what needs to get done and keep you accountable.

I NEED MY ALARM TO ACTUALLY WAKE ME!

Sleeping through your alarm? Try moving your alarm farther away from your bed, such as onto a bedroom desk or dresser. This requires you to get up from bed to turn off the alarm . . . and, well, now you're up, so you might as well just stay up and get ready for school!

MASTER HOMEWORK

Homework isn't always fun, but it *is* an opportunity to learn, practice skills, and boost your grades.

SET UP

- Designate a quiet, well-lit space in your home with a desk or a table to do your homework (rather than on the floor or in your bed).

- Store necessary supplies in your homework spot (pens, pencils, paper, scissors, correction fluid, markers, colored pencils, computer, charger).

- Set a schedule for yourself—this can help (see page 83).

- Use the ideas from Set Up for School Success (see page 84) as a guide. Learning to prioritize, follow through, and avoid distractions will help you with your homework.

GET GOING

1. Read the directions to understand your teacher's expectations for the assignment.

2. Complete the assignment. Ask for help if you need it.

3. If you are handing in the assignment, store it in a folder and put it in your backpack so you don't forget it. If you are submitting the work online, follow the directions and hit Submit.

ASK FOR HELP

It's normal to feel frustrated or uncertain or uncomfortable as you learn. It's also normal and okay to have questions, not understand, or be unable to complete a task. This is all part of the learning process. The good news is that others—teachers, caregivers, and classmates—can help.

1. Ask yourself, *What do I need?*

2. Find time to talk to a trusted adult, such as after class, or after dinner.

3. Be polite and direct about what you need. For example, *"Hi, Mrs. Smith, I was wondering if this was a good time for you to help me with last night's homework assignment. I was confused and need help figuring it out."*

4. Sometimes a teacher or caregiver doesn't have time to help. You can ask if there's a better time to talk or find another person to ask (even a classmate might be able to help). No matter what, keep asking until you get the help you need.

Be kind to yourself as you develop this skill. If you are nervous, that's okay. All feelings are allowed, but you don't have to let your nervousness or frustration stop you from asking for help.

RESOLVE CONFLICTS WITH AUTHORITY FIGURES

Conflicts occur when individuals have different ideas, opinions, beliefs, or feelings that lead to disagreement. Hopefully, everyone can express their perspective and also listen to the other person's perspective. Once everyone has been heard, the goal is to work together on a solution or a way to move forward.

For example, your teacher says you are talking too much during class. You disagree. You feel that you have been working hard and you only talk when there's a break in the lesson or before class starts. So what do you do?

1. Listen to the teacher's concerns and try to understand their perspective.

2. Share your perspective with the teacher, such as *"Your class is important to me. I want to learn. I also like to talk to my friends. I thought I was only doing it during breaks. I didn't realize you felt it was too much."*

3. Offer a suggestion that might help resolve the conflict. *"Is it okay if I talk with my friends before you start the lesson? My best friend is in the class, so it's hard not to speak to her, but I promise to work on talking less."*

Thank the other person for their time and perspective; hopefully they'll thank you, too!

CHAPTER 7
FRIENDS, THROUGH BETTER AND WORSE

- HAVE A GOOD CONVERSATION

- SHOW EMPATHY

- APOLOGIZE

- RESOLVE CONFLICTS

- SET AND KEEP HEALTHY BOUNDARIES

- DEAL WITH GROUP CONFLICTS

- USE SOCIAL MEDIA WISELY

- ENJOY TIME ALONE

HAVE A GOOD CONVERSATION

The key to being a good conversationalist is to listen *and build.* First, really listen to what someone is telling you. Then think to yourself, *How can I build on what this person has told me? Can I ask a follow-up question? Can I add my own observation or comment that relates to them?* Listening and building results in better and more interesting conversations.

HOW TO ACTIVELY LISTEN

1. Turn toward the speaker. Keep your eyes on them.

2. Create an image in your mind of what they are saying. This will help you remember what you're being told. Imagine yourself in the other person's shoes. This will help you to build understanding and empathy.

3. Think of follow-up questions, connections, or observations (like *What happened next? How did that make you feel?*).

4. Let the person finish speaking before you respond.

HOW TO HAVE A HARD CONVERSATION

Keep these strategies in mind as you initiate a difficult conversation.

- Find the appropriate moment. Don't catch people when they are distracted or stressed, rushing somewhere, or surrounded by others. Let them know that you want to talk with them and suggest a time and location.

- Have the conversation when you and the other person are calm. Don't attempt hard conversations when either of you is emotional, tired, or hungry.

- Begin by sharing your perspective. Focus on the facts you know and how the situation has made you feel. Be clear about what you want from this conversation, whether it is an apology, an opportunity to explain something, or steps to be taken to fix a situation.

- Ask the individual to share their perspective and feelings. Be ready to listen. Keep an open mind.

- If you think the conversation is resolved, consider closing with *"I'm so glad we had a chance to talk. I think we understand each other much better now."* Sometimes, you may not find a resolution, but you feel the conversation has reached a conclusion. In that case, try closing the conversation with *"Thank you for letting me share. It doesn't look like we are going to agree, but it's important that we both had an opportunity to explain our feelings."*

SHOW EMPATHY

Empathy is the ability to understand the feelings, experiences, and perspectives of other people. Have you heard the expression "Put yourself in their shoes"? That's what empathy is all about. It's imagining yourself in another person's position and showing compassion and support to a person who needs it. Empathy strengthens relationships, reduces conflict, and contributes to an all-around kinder, happier environment, whether that's in your home, classroom, or friend group.

- Listen carefully when people share their feelings or experiences.

- Don't be quick to judge someone's words or actions. Make sure you understand the full story. Consider how you would react to the same situation before you pass judgment on how another person behaves.

- Ask caring questions to show your interest and concern.

- Observe your surroundings and think of ways you can be helpful. Is someone telling you they feel left out? Do you notice someone sitting alone at lunch? Or looking lonely at recess? You can ask this person to hang out, introduce them to your friends, or strike up a conversation.

APOLOGIZE

Apologies can be hard. They can also be powerful. Giving a good apology can save a relationship and make you both feel better.

1. Be specific and take responsibility. Say, *"I'm sorry I yelled at you on the soccer field."*

2. Explain what happened, without excuses: *"I felt really frustrated, but it's not okay for me to take it out on my teammates."*

3. Express sincerity and remorse: *"I feel bad that I hurt your feelings, and I'm embarrassed that I lost my temper."*

4. If possible, offer to make amends. For example, if you've damaged or broken something, can you fix or replace it?

RESPOND TO AN APOLOGY

The simplest response to a good apology is often just *"Thank you for apologizing."* If you're still feeling upset, you can say, *"Thanks for the apology. I need time to think about it."* Or even *"Your apology makes me feel that you don't understand how much my feelings were hurt."*

ASK FOR AN APOLOGY

1. Arrange to talk privately.

2. Explain the situation and your feelings. Use I-statements, like *"I felt hurt when . . ."*

3. Ask for an apology and explanation. *"Why did you leave me out? I'd feel better with an apology and an explanation."*

RESOLVE CONFLICTS

Conflict is part of life. At some point, you will run into conflict with friends, parents, and teachers. It's important to address conflicts so they don't negatively impact your relationships or your well-being. Clearing the air and resolving a conflict feels better than avoiding the issue, which can magnify the problem or cause other conflicts.

1. **Calm down.** Make sure you're calm before starting the conversation. If you're feeling strong emotions, take a walk or some slow, deep breaths.

2. **State the conflict as you see it.** Let others know how the situation has made you feel using I-statements. For example, *"I noticed that you didn't ask me to sit at your lunch table. I felt really left out."*

3. **Ask for insight.** Ask the other person if they see the situation differently. What's their perspective?

4. **Apologize if needed.** If you discover you have done something wrong, take responsibility. *"I'm sorry I yelled at you after class. I was feeling frustrated, and I totally lost it. It's not okay, and I'm sure it made you feel bad. I understand why you didn't want to sit with me at lunch."*

5. **Offer solutions.** *"I'll be careful not to yell at you again. If I ever do something to upset you, please tell me right away so we can figure it out on the spot."*

6. **Get help if needed.** If a conflict escalates or feels as if it could become unsafe, get help from a trusted adult. Your safety and the safety of people around you is the most important thing, so always listen to your gut if it's telling you that a situation is getting out of hand or dangerous.

SET AND KEEP HEALTHY BOUNDARIES

A boundary is a limit you set with yourself or another person. Sometimes you set a boundary, and other times people set a boundary with you. Here are examples:

- **Boundary set by others for you:** Your caregivers won't allow you to go on Snapchat until you're 13.

- **Boundary set by you for others:** You don't let people you don't know well hug you.

- **Boundary set by you for you:** You put your phone in another room while doing homework.

Boundaries are important to your comfort, safety, and well-being. They also require practice and, sometimes, speaking up.

1. When you notice you're feeling uncomfortable or something isn't working for you, ask yourself, *What's bothering me? What do I need? Is there a boundary I can set?*

2. Decide on your boundary. This might require you to communicate it to others.

3. Stick to it. You may feel uncomfortable enforcing your boundary, or another person might feel upset by your boundary. This is normal. You can keep your boundary.

Boundaries are part of healthy relationships. If someone sets a boundary with you, that's helpful. It tells you what they expect. So your caregivers don't allow Snapchat. You know if you use Snapchat, there will be a consequence. You might not like it (and that's okay), but it helps to know what the limits are.

Likewise, just because someone asks you to do something or go somewhere doesn't mean you need to give consent (agree to it). For example, a friend might ask to copy your homework answers. You say no because that's a boundary you have set. If she responds that she doesn't want to sit with you at lunch, then she has set a boundary, too. You probably won't like it. You might feel upset. But at the same time, you can still stick with your boundary because it's important to you.

DEAL WITH GROUP CONFLICTS

Conflicts are a normal part of life. We all have our own experiences, feelings, ideas, and needs, so it makes sense that you sometimes might disagree with your friends or family.

Here's how conflict resolution works:

1. You notice you're feeling upset or uncomfortable. Maybe someone said or did something that bothered you.

2. Ask yourself, *How do I feel?* and *What do I need?*

3. When you're ready, communicate. Listen and share.

4. Work together to figure out how you can move forward.

EXAMPLE:

1. You weren't invited to a party with your friends.

2. You feel hurt. You need to express yourself.

3. You tell your friends how you're feeling. Your friends tell you the host was only allowed to invite four people. You explain that your feelings were still hurt.

4. You all agree to keep sharing your concerns and understand that sometimes everyone can't be included. You're disappointed but understand they didn't mean to hurt you and hope to include you next time.

PEER PRESSURE

Peer pressure is when you feel pressured to do or say something by other people your age. Sometimes peer pressure is positive, like if your friends pressure you to volunteer together. It can also be negative, pressuring you to do or say something that doesn't feel right to you. In this case, pause and think about how to respond. Here are some options:

- Walk away, get a drink, or go do something else.

- Move near someone who makes you feel more comfortable.

- Change the subject. If the group is talking negatively about someone, bring up plans you all have for the weekend.

- Set a boundary like *"I'm not comfortable with that party Friday, so I'm not going. Hopefully we can hang out Saturday."*

- Talk with a trusted adult. Negative peer pressure can be scary, and an adult perspective might reassure you and help you make decisions that fit with your values.

USE SOCIAL MEDIA WISELY

Social media helps you connect, learn, explore, share, and have fun—*and* it's entertaining. At the same time, social media has challenges that you need to pay attention to in order to use it wisely.

SAFETY

- Beware of communicating with people you haven't met—sometimes people aren't who they seem to be. Never agree to meet someone you've only met online. Don't answer messages from someone you don't know or send photos to people you don't know.

- Personal information should never be shared on social media. Keep your last name, address, school name, phone number, birthday, where you're going on vacation, and other personal information offline.

- Tell a trusted adult if you feel uncomfortable or something seems off.

ETIQUETTE

- Before you post or email a picture or comment, ask yourself if it's true, necessary, and kind.

- It's not always possible to delete messages or posts. Before you post or email, make sure it's something you're really okay with. Remember that whatever you post online is forever (even if deleted). When you apply for a job, the employer may check your social media to find out more about you.

- If someone posts a comment or picture that upsets you, talk with the person offline. It's okay to ask someone to take a picture down or tell them that their post hurt your feelings.

MENTAL HEALTH

- Social media is fun, but it's also important to spend time in "real life," achieving goals, having fun with friends in person, and trying new things.

- Too much technology isn't good for your brain. Using your brain and body in a variety of ways leads to greater health, well-being, and success.

- Remember that not everything you see online is true. Misleading and untruthful information is everywhere. And many people post what they want others to see and believe, so that everything looks perfect in their world— which it never is.

- If something online bothers you, tell a trusted adult or friend.

ENJOY TIME ALONE

Did you know that spending time alone doing what makes you happy leads to greater well-being and confidence? It's true! You learn more about yourself, who you are, and what you need. You might discover that you love being creative or are a good problem-solver. There's no right or wrong way to spend your alone time. This is the gift: You get to figure out what you need and what works for you.

- Use the time to do something you love—it could be drawing, reading, listening to music, organizing your room, practicing your basketball shot or your instrument, whatever. It could also be nothing—just chilling out, cuddling under your favorite blanket, or daydreaming. This is *your* time. Maybe hang a Do Not Disturb sign so you don't get interrupted.

- Especially after school, you probably just want a break to recharge before plunging into homework or after-school activities. Research shows that refreshing yourself with short, timed breaks energizes your body and brain and helps you be more productive when you return to your work. So, by all means, take a break: have a snack, spend time with your pet, get some fresh air, chat or text with a friend or family member.

WHAT DO I DO WHEN THE FEELING ISN'T MUTUAL?

Someone wants to be friends with you, but you don't want to be friends with them. This can feel uncomfortable. But it's okay to not be friends with everyone. You can be friendly without being friends. Setting an intention is helpful. For example, decide *I'll be kind and chat when we see each other at school, but not invite the other person to come over to my home.* This allows you to be kind to them *and* yourself.

PART THREE
OUT IN THE WORLD

As you grow older, you will naturally be more curious and ready to explore the world around you. This is an opportunity to try new things, interact with new people, and develop new skills. In Part 3, we'll explore the skills that will set you up for success as you become more independent. The best way to have more freedom is to take on more responsibility. You've got this!

CHAPTER 8
MONEY MAKES THE WORLD GO ROUND

- SPEND WISELY

- SAVE WISELY

- BUDGET

- UNDERSTAND AND MANAGE A BANK ACCOUNT

- LEAVE A TIP

- DONATE

SPEND WISELY

Got some money? It's natural to want to start shopping right away. But before you hit the stores, consider these suggestions.

- **Put needs before treats.** Prioritize "need-to-have" items before "nice-to-have" items. If there's money left over after you've purchased what you need and set aside savings, then feel confident buying the fun extras.

- **Do your homework.** If there's an item you really want, don't buy the first one you see. Check if other stores offer this item at a lower price and find out if it ever goes on sale. A savvy shopper looks for deals!

- **Beware of advertising.** Businesses use smart, targeted advertising to lure customers to their products. Before purchasing something, decide if you truly want the item or you are falling for seductive branding and advertising. Consider whether this product will really live up to its promise and fit your needs.

- **Keep track of spending.** You can learn a lot about your spending patterns by writing them down. For example, are you spending most of your money on vending machine snacks? Could you save money by bringing these snacks from home or buying them in bulk from the grocery store? Keeping track of your spending helps you make smarter saving and spending decisions.

SAVE WISELY

It's fun to spend money on things you want. Having your own money gives you independence, which is exciting. However, being independent and financially responsible also means learning to save. And saving money isn't as easy as spending it.

Learning a few simple saving habits will pay off when you have enough money to splurge on something really special, make a donation to a meaningful cause, or pay your own expenses.

Saving money also helps you prepare for unexpected situations, like if you accidentally break a neighbor's window with a lacrosse ball!

- **Think about how much you want to save and spend.** One good rule is to save at least 10 percent of your earnings. You might want to save even more aggressively, especially if you're saving toward something specific. In that case, consider saving 50 percent and allowing yourself to spend the other half. Some kids divide their earnings into even thirds for saving, spending, and charitable donations.

- **Aim for the future.** If you don't spend money on little items now, you'll have more money for bigger items later. Think back to what you need and what you want, and focus on buying what you need now so you can save enough money to buy what you want later.

- **Keep your money in a secure place** at home and consider opening a bank account where your savings can earn interest (see page 112).

- **Check out apps that help kids learn to budget and save.** And look into having automatic deductions from your paycheck (if you have one) or bank account directed into a savings account. An automatic deduction makes saving easy: Just set it and forget it!

BUDGET

A budget is a plan for spending and saving. Learning to budget is a valuable life skill: It sets you up for financial success in the future.

1. To develop a budget, start by figuring out how much money you earn regularly, such as your allowance or money from a job.

2. Record all your regular expenses, like daily snacks, and your expected occasional expenses, like holiday gifts. Write down the total of all your expenses.

3. Divide your expenses into categories so you can see how much money you're spending on certain items (like clothes and hangouts with friends).

4. Now match what you earn with what you spend. If you're spending more than you earn, get sneaky with cuts. Let's say your weekly cash is $15, but your expenses are $20. Could packing your snacks once a week make a difference? If you can spend less, congratulate yourself and save the extra money. Piling up these extra bucks will help you manage bigger expenses and unexpected purchases.

5. Work on the "Save Wisely" skillset (page 108) to set and reach your financial goals and build good spending habits for the future.

UNDERSTAND AND MANAGE A BANK ACCOUNT

When you have a bank account and manage your money well, you have the freedom to pay for the things that you want and need to do. It's a big, empowering step toward independence!

SETTING UP AN ACCOUNT

You can set up a custodial bank account with a trusted adult. You might want a checking account that lets you write checks and withdraw cash, and a savings account that lets you store and build on the money you're not using.

DEBIT CARD

With your new account, you may receive a debit card that lets you spend the money you have in your account. (With a credit card, you borrow money that you pay back to the credit card company at a later date.) You can use your debit card to make purchases or get cash from your account.

ATM

ATM stands for "automated teller machine." You can use this machine to deposit or withdraw money using your debit card or check how much money you have in your account.

When you set up your bank account, you will choose a four-digit security code called a PIN (personal identification number), so you can access your account using your debit card.

To use an ATM, insert your card in the machine, follow the screen directions to complete your transaction, and be sure to get your card back!

It's usually best to use the ATM at your own bank. You can find ATMs at other banks and stores, but they may charge fees.

ONLINE SECURITY

- Create strong, unique passwords for your accounts. Change your passwords every three months.

- Never share personal information like your username, social security number, or account number unless you initiate the contact. The bank will never ask you to tell them your password directly.

- Don't use shared devices or networks to access your bank account.

- Check your account regularly for unauthorized use.

LEAVE A TIP

A tip is a way to thank someone for their service. Hairdressers, waiters, taxi drivers, and food delivery drivers are just some of the service professionals who receive tips.

- Customers generally tip 15 to 20 percent of the bill. So if you spend $10 on a meal, for example, and want to leave a 15 percent tip, you would leave $1.50. If the service was great, you might give 20 percent, which in this case would be $2.00. The better the service, the higher the tip.

- You decide how much you would like to leave. But remember: Tips are important because this is partly how a person gets paid for the work they do.

To figure out a tip, use your math skills. Say the bill is $12.50. Get rid of the last number (in this case, the 0)—this gives you 125 (or $1.25). That's 10 percent. For every 10 percent, you add another 125. So 20 percent would be 250 (or $2.50).

DONATE

Donating money gives you an opportunity to help other people, animals, and society. It feels good to support others in need.

- **Think about a cause.** If you like animals, you could give money to your local animal shelter or the World Wildlife Fund. If you want to help feed the hungry, you could buy food for your local food pantry or donate to Feeding America or Action Against Hunger. What other topics interest you? The environment? Education? Mental health?

- **Do a little research.** Find an organization that you want to help. Check out charitynavigator.org to make sure that most of the donated money goes directly to the intended recipients. You can also ask a trusted adult for help with this.

- **Give.** With an adult's help, send the organization money for their goals or needs. You can donate through the mail, online, or in person.

- **Consider making a commitment.** People donate anywhere from 1 to 5 percent of their income to charity, though any amount is welcome. If you made $500 babysitting over the year, you could give anywhere from $5–25 to charity if you wanted.

I'M READY TO WORK. WHERE DO I START?

Get creative! Think about your skills and what you enjoy doing. Perhaps you like playing with younger children. If so, babysitting is a great way to make money. Maybe you'd like to do yard work, wash cars, walk dogs, or feed pets while their families are away. Or tutor a younger child in math. Or help people learn how to use their computer. Make flyers and distribute them to friends and neighbors you know. Ask your caregiver for advice about fees and safety first.

CHAPTER 9
SAY WHAT YOU MEAN, MEAN WHAT YOU SAY

- COMMUNICATE ONLINE

- MAKE AND RECEIVE PHONE CALLS

- TEXT WITH CARE

- EMAIL WITH CARE

- WRITE A THANK-YOU NOTE

- USE GOOD MANNERS

COMMUNICATE ONLINE

Think about the internet like a giant playground. It's an exciting place to explore, and there are lots of opportunities for fun. But you also have to be careful and stay safe.

- **Protect your password.** Your passwords are secret codes that unlock your online stuff. Never share passwords with anyone. Your BFF might be super trustworthy, but everyone makes mistakes, and you don't want your passwords falling into the wrong hands. Keep 'em safe and keep 'em to yourself. Change your passwords often; use numbers, symbols, and capital and lowercase letters; and don't include information that others can guess, like your birthday.

- **Be wary with strangers.** We've talked about how not everyone is who they say they are. Don't chat with people that you haven't met in person unless you check with a trusted adult first. And if anything feels off, tell your adult right away, even if you think you'll get in trouble. Your safety comes first.

- **Keep personal info private.** Don't tell just anyone your home address. Don't post pictures or videos wearing clothing that advertises your town. Only share your personal information—such as age, address, and location—with people you really know and trust. Let an adult know right away if anyone asks you for this information.

- **Consider before you click.** Sometimes a cool link or ad might pop up while you're online. Before you click, check that the link looks safe and legit. If you're not sure, check with an adult.

- **Think before you "speak."** Sometimes, when people are not face-to-face, it's easier for them to say things that are hurtful. Before communicating anything online, it's helpful to THINK about your message:

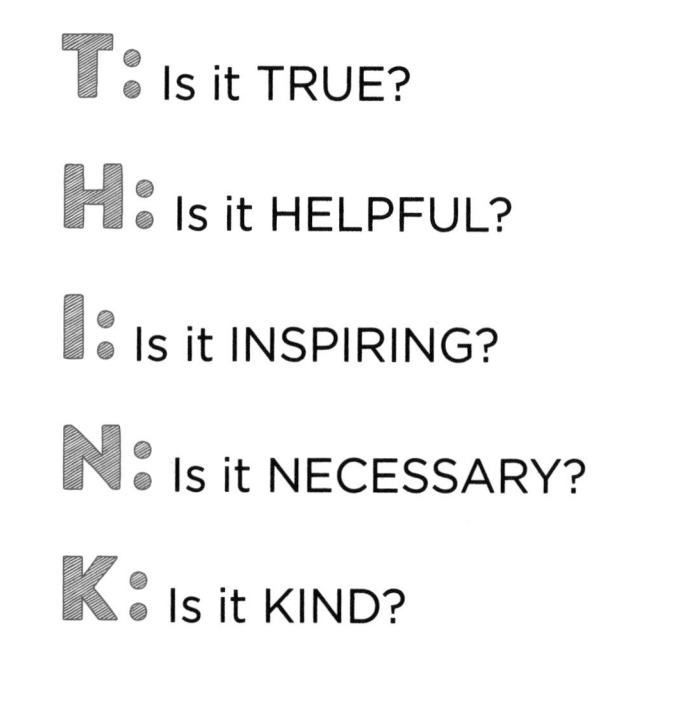

T: Is it TRUE?

H: Is it HELPFUL?

I: Is it INSPIRING?

N: Is it NECESSARY?

K: Is it KIND?

MAKE AND RECEIVE PHONE CALLS

These days you may be texting more often than talking, but sometimes a phone conversation happens, and the way you handle it shows a lot about you as a person. Here are a few "best practices" for making and receiving phone calls.

TO MAKE A PHONE CALL

1. Move to a quiet place.

2. Dial the phone number.

3. When someone picks up, start with a greeting. If the person you're calling has their own number, you can greet this individual by name. Say who you are.

4. If you need to speak to another person, you can say something like *"Hi, this is _____. May I please speak with _____ ?"* or *"Hi, Uncle Ray. I'm calling to wish Aunt Helen a happy birthday. Is she there?"*

5. State your purpose for calling. Speak clearly.

6. Wrap up the conversation with a message of appreciation like *"Thanks for speaking with me."* Then say goodbye and hang up.

7. If no one answers, leave a short message with your name, the time you called, what you wanted to talk about, and your phone number so they can call you back.

TO RECEIVE A PHONE CALL

- When the phone rings, you can answer by saying, *"Hello?"* Or if you know who's calling, open with *"Hi, _____!"* From here, it's often nice to continue by asking *"How are you?"*

- When the conversation finishes, you may want to end by saying, *"Thanks for calling. Bye!"*

TEXT WITH CARE

Text messaging is a fast and easy way to communicate, with a few important considerations.

- Never text with someone you don't know. If you get a text from an unknown person, ignore it or say "wrong person." If they keep texting, block them.

- Texting differs from voice conversations in one important way: What you write is permanent. And thanks to screenshots, your text may not always stay private. So never text anything that you wouldn't say to someone's face. Ask yourself, *Is this text something that I'd be okay with my grandma reading?* If the answer is no, you probably shouldn't send it.

- Be careful about sending photos of yourself or others—they could be misused. Don't take or send a photo of someone else without their permission.

- When you speak with someone, you can see their facial expressions and body language and hear their tone of voice. All of this is missing with texting, and that opens the possibility of misunderstanding, no matter how clear you thought your message was. Be extra careful what you type. Use emojis to make your intentions clearer.

- Read and reread your texts before sending. Remember, you can't take back what you sent.

- Don't text when you're angry or frustrated or upset. You can't take back those messages, either.

- Don't send messages too early in the morning or late at night.

EMAIL WITH CARE

Email is an effective and necessary communication tool. You might send an email to a teacher, coach, grandparent, person you are working for (or want to work for), or friend. These guidelines will help you come across as the thoughtful person you are!

1. Write an interesting subject line that is related to the purpose of your email and will capture the reader's attention.

2. Use an appropriate greeting like *Dear Ms. Smith; Hi, Aunt Katy;* or *Hey, Sarah!* depending on your relationship to the person you're writing.

3. Write a clear message communicating the purpose of your email.

4. Use a closing remark and then your name. Examples of closing remarks include *Thank you* or *Sincerely,* or in the case of a close friend, *See you later!*

5. Check your grammar and spelling and make sure you're sending it to the right person before you press Send.

6. Like texting, don't send emails when you are angry, frustrated, or upset. You can't take those words back.

WRITE A THANK-YOU NOTE

Sending a thank-you note is a meaningful way to express your gratitude to another person.

1. Use an appropriate greeting like *Dear Ms. Jones* or *Hi, Jane!*

2. Write a brief note expressing your gratitude for the gift, assistance, or kind act. Explain how their kindness made you feel. If it's for a gift, include your plans for using the gift.

3. Add a closing remark and then your name. Examples of closing remarks include *Thank you again* or *Sincerely*.

EXAMPLE:

Dear Chloe,

Thank you for the amazing sweatshirt. I can't wait to wear it to school and will think of you when I wear it. It was so kind of you to give me something special for my birthday.

Thank you,

(Your name)

ADDRESS AN ENVELOPE

There are usually three lines to include when you address an envelope: 1. the recipient's name; 2. their street address (and any unit number), and 3. city, state, and zip code. Use the two-letter state abbreviation.

Write the address in the middle of the envelope. Place a stamp in the upper right-hand corner of the envelope. In the upper left corner, write your name, street address, and city, state, and zip code. This will help the post office return your letter in case it can't be delivered.

Letters to another country require extra postage. These addresses also look different depending on the country, so be sure you have the correct and complete address. Ask for the right stamps for that country at the post office.

USE GOOD MANNERS

Using good manners shows that you respect yourself and others. They help cement your reputation as a courteous person. They encourage others to treat you the same way. And they help you get what you want.

- **Remember please and thank you.** When asking for something, saying "please" communicates a need and shows you are polite and appreciative, and it's more likely to get you what you want than "I need this." Likewise, saying "thank you" acknowledges what that person did for you.

- **Start with a good handshake.** Many people shake hands to say hello or end a conversation. A firm handshake shows confidence and sincerity. Not everyone shakes hands, though—just be ready in case someone extends their hand.

  1. While standing, extend your right hand so the other person can easily grasp it.

  2. Smile and look the person in the eye as you shake their hand.

  3. Hold their hand firmly (but not too tightly!) and move your hand up and down with theirs. Let go.

- **Use eye contact.** Eye contact communicates confidence, kindness, and interest. The idea is to look someone in the eye comfortably without staring. Practice in a mirror.

- **Resist interrupting.** Unless there's an emergency, always let people finish talking before responding.

- **Respect boundaries.** Give people their personal space. Keep a reasonable distance away from others in conversation and in line.

- **Ask for consent.** Don't assume that others want what you want. For example, ask them if you can give them a hug or show them something.

- **Practice good table manners.** Wait until everyone at the table is served before you begin eating. Ask for items to be passed to you, rather than reaching for them. Compliment the food and thank the person who made the meal. Offer to help clean up. You'll surely get invited back!

- **Hold the door for the person behind you.** Nobody likes a door slammed in their face! Be kind and hold the door open for whoever is following you in or out of a building.

I HATE TO ASK, BUT . . . !

Asking for a favor can feel awkward. But everyone needs help once in a while. If you can ask others for favors (without overdoing it!), they will feel comfortable asking for your help, too, and that feels good!

- First, acknowledge that the person you're asking might be busy. Say, *"Hey, I know you have a lot going on . . ."* Or if you're asking to borrow something, acknowledge how this item might be special or something the person uses often. This shows you understand that granting you this favor is a kindness.

- State what you need. For example, *"I'm working on the Spanish project, and I don't understand the directions. Can you please help me with this?"*

- Finally, show your gratitude for the person's time, effort, or generosity. *"Thanks so much. I really appreciate it! If I can ever repay the kindness . . ."*

CHAPTER 10
OUT AND ABOUT

- READ A MAP

- PACK A SUITCASE

- HOST A HANGOUT

- BE A GREAT GUEST

- WATCH A YOUNGER CHILD

- PICK AND WRAP A PRESENT

- MAKE SMART DECISIONS

READ A MAP

Sure, you probably use an app to find places. But there might come a day when you'll need to use an old-fashioned map to navigate a route on a road trip or hiking trail.

1. Orient yourself with the entire map. Identify the compass rose, which shows the directions of north, south, east, and west. When you hold a map, match the north on the map to the actual north direction.

2. Locate your starting point.

3. Find your destination using landmarks printed directly on the map.

4. Review your journey before you begin. You'll be less likely to take a wrong turn if you know where you're going.

5. Get familiar with the legends and symbols in the map key that represent roads, rivers, parks, cities, and landmarks. Use the symbols you need for your trip.

6. Maps use scale to relate distance on the map to real-world distance. For example, one inch on the map might represent one mile in reality. Using this system, calculate your total mileage by measuring the distance between your starting point and destination.

Getting lost can be frustrating and even frightening. If you find yourself in an unfamiliar place, try the following strategies:

- Pause and collect your thoughts. Gather information about your surroundings, such as recognizable landmarks. Look at your map to retrace the steps that brought you to this place.

- If necessary, find a trusted adult, such as a police officer or store employee, and explain that you're lost and need help. Never go with a stranger who offers help.

- Bring important information or better yet, have it memorized. Know your caregivers' cell phone numbers by heart so you can give other people these numbers or make a call for help.

- If someone is looking for you, stay where you are and be visible. Wandering around can make it more challenging for someone to find you.

PACK A SUITCASE

Ooh, you're going somewhere—fun! One way to approach packing is to visualize your body from head to toe. What will you need to wear on your head? Your upper body? Your legs? Your feet? Consider the weather at your destination and how many days you'll be traveling. Pack clean clothing for each day, unless you know you'll have access to a washer and dryer. You can wear pants and sweaters more than once, but bring fresh socks and underwear for every day you're away. Here's a checklist.

FEET
- Socks
- Shoes: Will you need sneakers? Flip-flops? Dressy shoes? Boots?

BOTTOMS
- Underwear
- Pants/shorts/skirts

TOPS

- Shirts: Will you need short or long sleeves? Some of each?
- Sweater/sweatshirt: No matter where you're going, you might be happy to have an extra layer of warmth!
- Coat

MISCELLANEOUS

- Pajamas
- A more formal or dressy outfit
- Bathing suit
- Chargers
- A good book
- Games

TOILETRIES (IN A TOILETRY BAG)

(If carrying a bag onto a plane, liquids and gels typically must be 3.4 ounces or less)

- Toothbrush/toothpaste
- Hairbrush
- Deodorant
- Tampons/pads
- Face cleanser and moisturizer
- Contact lenses and accessories
- Eyeglasses

When packing a suitcase, try rolling your clothing up neatly and tuck each item tightly against one another in the suitcase. This will create space and minimize wrinkling.

Place shoes in a plastic bag and pack at the bottom of the suitcase, or tuck them along the sides of the suitcase with the soles facing away from your clothing. This will protect your clean clothes.

Finally, place the items you think you'll need first at the top, so when you arrive at your destination, you don't need to rummage around to find what you need. For example, pack your toiletry bag and pajamas on top in case you arrive late and want to hop into bed right away!

HOST A HANGOUT

Hosting a hangout can be really fun, and it's a great way to connect with friends. Here are ways you can prepare an easy, casual get-together.

1. **Invite the right mix.** Think about everyone's personalities and how they would get along. Sometimes a big group can be overwhelming or difficult to control, so maybe keep it small. Consider whether you're leaving anyone out and how this might make that person feel.

2. **Plan for a hungry crowd.** If you're hosting an event at mealtime, plan to have something substantial to feed your guests. Pizza, sandwiches, hot dogs, and hamburgers are crowd pleasers. Even if it's not mealtime, guests will look for snacks, like bowls of chips and salsa, hummus and veggies, or desserts. Consider any food allergies.

3. **Plan activities.** What are your guests going to do? This could be making a craft, playing games, watching a movie, painting—whatever! Activities give everyone something to do and make conversation easier. It's okay if the group abandons the activity; maybe a better idea came up or the conversation is going so well that you don't need the activity.

4. **Make a shopping list.** Think about plates, napkins, food, drinks, craft supplies—whatever you think you'll need.

5. **Invite your guests.** Set a date and start and end time, and share the details with your guests.

6. **Prepare the space.** Clean the area where you'll be hanging out. Make sure there are plenty of seats.

7. **Greet your friends.** Welcome them at the door and introduce guests who don't know each other.

8. **Enjoy and host.** Mingle and check on your guests to make sure they're enjoying the get-together and have what they need.

9. **Wrap it up.** Walk each guest to the door and thank them for coming.

10. **Clean up.** Put everything back in its place and thank your caregivers. They'll appreciate how responsible you are and hopefully agree to more hangouts!

BE A GREAT GUEST

Being a guest is an opportunity to connect with friends at their home. You can get to know them better and see what their home life is all about.

1. Wait for your friend to invite you over. If it's for a party, accept the invitation as soon as possible and offer to bring something to eat or drink.

2. Ask your friend before you arrive how to address the adults in the home. For example, *"Does your mom like to be called Mrs. Smith or something else?"*

3. Ask if you should take your shoes off at the door.

4. Say hello to everyone and treat family members or other friends in the home with kindness and respect.

5. Act appropriately. Take cues from your friend. If your friend puts their dishes in the sink after dinner, do the same. If you are unsure about what is allowed or how to help, just ask.

6. Be respectful of their home. For example, if you spill something, offer to clean it up.

7. Remember to say please, thank you, and goodbye. These are the kinds of words that make a guest great!

WATCH A YOUNGER CHILD

Babysitting a younger child is a privilege. It builds maturity, shows responsibility, and is a great way to gain experience and earn money or help your caregivers by looking after your little sibling. Here are ways to responsibly care for someone younger.

- **Stay watchful.** If you're playing outside, watch for oncoming traffic, make sure kids wear helmets if biking or riding a scooter, and stay close to them. Indoors, make sure they don't put small objects into their mouth, keep them away from hot surfaces, and stay close while they are eating, near water, or on stairs.

- **Remember allergies and choking hazards.** Never give children anything to eat unless their adults have approved it. Be aware of any food allergies and know that some foods can cause choking in young children.

- **Play with them.** Play games, use your imagination to have fun, and interact with them on their level.

- **Know important numbers.** Ask for the parents' cell phone numbers and an additional emergency contact (such as a neighbor), in case you cannot reach the parents. You can always call 911 with an emergency. If you're unsure whether or not you need emergency help, just make the call. It's better to be safe than sorry.

PICK AND WRAP A PRESENT

Picking out a thoughtful present and wrapping it beautifully is fun and shows you care.

- Do you share common interests? How about a present that reflects that?

- Make it a treat. Is there something they would like but wouldn't buy for themselves?

- How about a gift card for a service like a manicure or pedicure?

- Consider a gift you can share: a trip to a museum together, a hike, a movie.

- Gather a group of people to contribute to a bigger gift. If your friend is having a birthday party, pitch in for a gift with one or more other guests.

Putting your gift into a decorative bag with tissue paper is the easiest way to go, but what if you want to use wrapping paper instead? We've got you covered!

1. Place the present in a box, if possible.

2. Gather scissors, wrapping paper, and tape.

3. On a table, lay out a piece of wrapping paper, decorative side down. Place the box or item facedown in the center of the wrapping paper.

4. Cut the paper large enough to cover all sides of the gift.

5. Bring one side of the wrapping paper to the center of the gift and tape it down. Bring the other side up and over so it overlaps the other end. Tape it down.

6. One open side at a time, fold in the sides of the paper. Fold down the top center paper. Then fold up the bottom center paper. Tape shut.

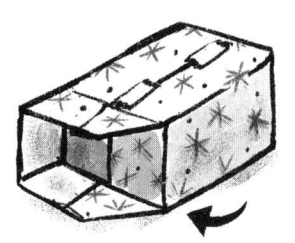

7. Repeat step 6 on the other side.

8. Turn the gift over so the taped side faces down. Add a bow and a card or tag, and you're done!

MAKE SMART DECISIONS

As you grow up, you'll have many chances to make decisions for yourself. Making good decisions and solving problems can help you take control and succeed. Here are some steps to guide you.

1. **Identify the issue.** What is the challenge or choice you need to make? Be as detailed as possible.

2. **Brainstorm possibilities or solutions.** Explore several possibilities, even if some seem impossible. Just the act of brainstorming leads to more productive problem-solving and decision-making.

3. **Pick one or two options and explore.** Explore the potential benefits and consequences of each.

4. **Choose an option and take action.** Make your decision and run with it.

5. **Evaluate.** What went well? Is further action required?

LET'S GIVE IT A TRY!

1. Identify the issue: *You play volleyball and do cheerleading each fall, but their schedules conflict in your new school so you can't do both.*

2. Brainstorm possibilities or solutions:

   - *Attend a practice for each sport and see which looks like more fun.*

   - *Ask your friends which activity they are doing and why.*

   - *Talk to your caregiver and ask for their thoughts.*

   - *Find another volleyball league that won't interfere with cheer.*

   - *Sign up for both and hope for the best.*

3. Pick an option or two and explore: *You decide to talk to your caregiver. You know that talking to her makes you feel better. She also suggests looking into a volleyball league that meets in the winter so you can keep up your skills. You call the league and learn it's kind of expensive.*

4. Pick an option and take action: *You decide to stick with cheer and start saving babysitting money to help pay for volleyball.*

5. Evaluate: *You feel better. You can still do both. You'll need to keep saving if you want to play volleyball, but you can always choose to switch sports later.*

WALKING ALONE: HOW DO I STAY SAFE?

You want to walk to a friend's house, but she lives a few blocks away. Brainstorm ways to help yourself.

- Ask your caregiver for permission, so they know where you're going and when.

- Tell your friend you're coming and when to expect you.

- Walk on sidewalks or grass, especially on busy roads.

- If you have a phone, keep it in your pocket (don't text while walking) and observe your surroundings as you walk.

- Walk confidently. You might not feel confident, but you can walk as if you are. You can build confidence as you go. You've got this!

- Call or text your caregiver when you arrive at your friend's house.

If you're not ready (or allowed) to walk to a friend's house, that's okay! You can practice the walk with a caregiver for now.

ACKNOWLEDGMENTS

Thank you to Tahra Seplowin and the Zeitgeist division of Penguin Random House for sharing their vision with us and giving us the opportunity to write this book. To Susan Randol, our editor, for believing in us and guiding us through the process. To all of the teachers and administrators we worked with in Greenwich, Connecticut, and to those who taught us and our children in Rye, New York, we are grateful for your support, kindness, and inspiration. Thank you to all of our friends for listening, laughing, and supporting us throughout this process. And a very special thank-you to our families, whose support and love both inspire and ground us.

ABOUT THE AUTHORS

 **LISA QUIRK WEINMAN** is a cofounder of Middle Years Matter, an organization devoted to empowering young people with the essential skills needed to thrive academically, socially, and emotionally. She served as middle school dean of students and wellness teacher at an independent school in Greenwich, Connecticut, for 22 years. She lives in Rye, New York, with her husband and two boys.

 **MEGAN MONAGHAN** is a cofounder of Middle Years Matter and has worked in education for more than 18 years. She has taught every grade level from third to eighth grade. She holds degrees from Columbia University in child development and reading disabilities. She absolutely loves being a teacher. Megan lives in Rye, New York, with her family.

ABOUT THE ILLUSTRATOR

 **MARTHA SUE COURSEY** is a San Francisco–based illustrator, type designer, and artist. She grew up as the only child of metalwork artists in a house they built on the outskirts of Tucson, Arizona, where books and desert creatures were some of her best friends. She holds a BFA in painting from California College of the Arts and a postgraduate certificate from Type West. When she's not drawing, she's taking care of too many plants or walking the dog. For more information, visit marthasuecoursey.com.